SET PLAYS

organizing and coaching dead ball situations

by Marco Ceccomori

REEDSWAIN
PUBLISHING

Originally published in 2003 under the title *L'Allenamento e L'Organizzazione delle Situazioni Offensive e Difensive di Palla Inattiva* by:

www.allenatore.net
via E.Francalanci, 418
55050 Bozzano (LU)
Italia

**Library of Congress
Cataloging - in - Publication Data**

SET PLAYS
organizing and coaching
dead ball situations
Marco Ceccomori
ISBN No. 1-59164-084-9
Lib. of Congress Catalog No. 2004095456
© 2004

Art Direction, Layout and Proofing
Bryan R. Beaver

Translated by
Sinclair de Courcy Williams

Printed by
DATA REPRODUCTIONS
Auburn, Michigan

Reedswain Publishing
612 Pughtown Road
Spring City, PA 19475
800.331.5191
www.reedswain.com
info@reedswain.com

CONTENTS

INTRODUCTION

When listening to coaches and experts from the world of soccer commenting on a game, you often hear them say: 'Today's match was decided by a single episode.'

What they very often mean by the expression 'episode' is that a goal has been scored following on or because of a free kick.

The ability to make the most of set plays is without doubt a determining factor in the success of a team, both as regards a balanced match and also as a prerogative in itself.

It is evident that during a match in which the two sides balance themselves out in terms of play, the best use of kicks from stationary balls will often be crucial to the victory of one of the two teams.

Yet, looking more closely at statistics concerning the causes leading to scoring in soccer, we can note that goals that arise or develop directly from free kicks are of a very high percentage, varying from 40 to 50 %.

It is very important as a result for any coach in whatever category to dedicate a lot of his time to these particular playing situations, both in the attacking and in the defense phase.

This study is to be placed in such a context, and our aim is to supply an instrument of support, not to mention stimulating ideas to reflect on and investigate, which will be useful in the organization of this fundamental component in the game of soccer. We will not only be looking at the physical and tactical conditions on an individual and collective level, but also at aspects connected with the players' psychological make up and their character, as well as a huge case study of attacking and defense schemes to be used in the most important dead ball situations.

Marco Ceccomoro

FOREWORD

DEAD BALL SITUATIONS IN ATTACK

The following are the most important dead ball situations in the attacking phase, which we will begin by looking at in general and then go on to develop in each single case:

1) Kick off;
2) Keeper putting the ball back into play;
3) Free kicks;
4) Corner kicks;
5) Throw ins;
6) Penalty kicks.

If he wants to make the best of his team's ability to be productive in attack, it is vital for the coach to train his players in all the situations listed above.

It is not a good idea, particularly as far as youth teams are concerned, to limit yourself in coaching sessions to the continuous repetition of specific schemes. On the contrary, your methods must be preceded and accompanied by good training both in the technical and tactical aspects and in the principles that underlie these situations.

CHAPTER 1

GENERAL PRINCIPLES

Making the best use of your players' characteristics

Here we are talking about what I consider to be the most important point to be kept in mind. The coach's principle task is the study and evaluation of his players' characteristics, and this is vital to his choice of what each single player's role and assignment will be, just as it also underlies his decision to use a particular playing system instead of another.

Besides, this analysis is very important as concerns the structuring and organization of free kick situations.

In fact the coach's main aim will be to train his players in free kick solutions that will put their skills and abilities into light.

If you do not have good jumpers and headers in the group, it is no good, and will in fact be counterproductive, to set up restart plays that make use of high balls. In these cases it is better to structure movements that will send a player with a good driving kick to shoot on goal.

These are only a couple of examples to show how very important it is to give fluidity and organization to the attacking schemes used on free kicks which will make the best use of the players you have at hand.

Some people might say that all this is banal, but these things very often get lost because coaches complicate their lives and the lives of their players by looking for solutions that may, broadly speaking, be correct, but which are not very suitable for the characteristics of the team they are supposed to be directing.

Reading the situation of play

During a match the soccer player finds himself having to face countless playing situations to which he has to make suitable motorial responses.

In modern soccer, tactical decisions have to be made very quickly, and before he has even taken possession of the ball, the player must already have read the situation of play correctly and chosen the most suitable move to carry out.

Who is in possession? Where is the ball? Where are my teammates? And my opponents? Where is the goal?

These are some of the most important situation questions that the single player needs to repeat to himself at every moment of the match.

The coach's basic task is to give instruction to all his players on how to read and evaluate the various situations of play in the same way, so that a team is formed that 'thinks and acts in a collective way'.

The correct reading and interpretation of the context of play on the part of the players are vital factors even as far as set plays are concerned.

The players must grasp and assimilate the attacking plays to be developed from stationary balls, and the coach must look for and organize methods that will make that happen in dynamic, situational ways rather than closing things off and limiting the process.

The fact is that each single player will have to be coached in how to interpret variations in the context of play as quickly and as correctly as possible, so as to be in a position to choose the attacking solution that will be most suitable to the new situation.

We can say this from a global point of view: the more developed the team's responsiveness to situational play in a collective context, the more unpredictable and effective their natural actions will be on free kicks.

Surprise and unpredictability

Taken together, surprise and unpredictability represent fundamental principles in the correct collective build up of the attacking phase.

What you need are players who are full of imagination and creativity whose hunches will surprise and catch out the opponents' defense line up. In addition, the team as a whole will need to constantly vary its attacking solutions to make it more difficult for the opponents to set up instant and operational countermeasures in defense. Naturally, these concepts are valid for our particular subject as well.

Taking a free kick immediately before the wall has been correctly put into place, and a good assortment of solutions on corner kicks are only two practical examples.

It is to be underlined how the team's attitude in making the best use of surprise and unpredictability is directly proportionate to its ability to interpret playing situations as effectively as possible. Each new solution will come like a bombshell, and all the organized variations in playing schemes will turn out to be truly productive only if they are the fruit of an alert, accurate evaluation of the context of play.

Space and time

As we have already said, soccer is a situational sport, which means that the coach must be able in training to give useful instruments to his players, allowing them to read and evaluate the many situations of play that will appear on the field so as to get suitable technical and tactical responses in connection with the two most important variables in the game: SPACE and TIME.

In fact, one of the most important requirements in building up maneuvers that will be fluid and worthwhile is the players' ability to create and occupy space during the attacking phase with the right timing.

These concepts are also pertinent to the way you structure the team's organization on set plays.

It is very important, therefore, to coach your team in how to create and occupy space with the right timing even in relation to all dead ball situations. To put it more specifically, the coach must not only concentrate on the technical aspects of the kick itself, but should also coordinate the players' movements in relation to the resumption of play.

To do that you have to oversee the association between the player kicking the ball and his teammates whose job it is to make moves that will enable them to occupy space. When organizing these aspects, you very often work out a number of standard gestures (e.g., raising and lowering an arm) or even specific technical plays (a player touches the ball to a teammate who stops it with the sole of his boot), whose aim is to coordinate the movements and at the same time to give those who are to receive the ball time to attack the spaces as well as possible.

Mobility

Mobility is a vital collective factor in the attacking phase. Well-organized and coordinated movements without the ball among players carrying out an action in the attacking phase, timing it right and both creating and occupying space will allow you to build up play that gives no firm points of reference to the opponents.

You have to make continuous changes of position between teammates while still respecting the correct timing of play - and that will make it very difficult for the opponents to carry out marking.

Set plays are no exception to these concepts.

In order to create a real danger, it is vital that those who are to receive the pass from a stationary ball must make the necessary movements when not in possession.

Every movement to break free of marking must be carried out in order to create and occupy a promising, useful space, and it will have to be organized and coordinated with the movements of the teammates without the ball and with the kick itself..

Immobility and self-centeredness, then, are damaging things in relation to free kicks in the attacking phase, and it will be the coach's job to discourage and condemn such behavior.

In figure 1 there is a solution on a side free kick where player nº 8 exchanges with nº 7, who then crosses to the center for the teammates who get free of marking by attacking the spaces that they have created for each other.

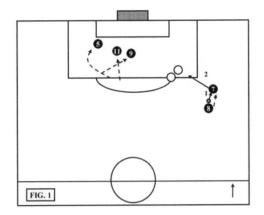

FIG. 1

Numerical superiority

Effective attacking plays will always aim to get and create numerical superiority.

An exchange of passes, dribbling and overlapping are only a few of the most important technical and tactical methods used to create numerical superiority, and they are indispensable to building up a fluid, efficient and productive attacking phase.

Looking for and creating numerical superiority is just as important in reference to stationary balls.

Overlapping along the flank, releasing a player of marking and putting him in a position to cross after a free kick or an exchange of passes on a throw in are frequently used themes and can be very functional when you are trying to break a teammate out of marking.

In figure 2, player n° 7 goes above the ball to get free of marking along the flank and receives the pass from teammate n° 9, who has been served by n° 8's side free kick.

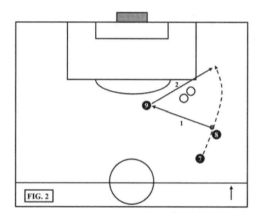

FIG. 2

Favorable individual duels

The results of matches very often depend on the advantage arising from the success of an individual duel. The game of soccer is made up of continuous 1 against 1 situations, and it is the coach's job to look for and organize favorable individual clashes.

By making careful and detailed examination of their individual characteristics, the coach will be able to pinpoint the positions and the tasks of those players in his group who are best able to take advantage of his opponents' weaknesses.

For example, in front of a slow side defender the coach should use a fast side attacking player who can use his speed to create problems for his direct adversary.

Exploiting the individual weaknesses of the opponents is very

11

important also as regards set plays.

If your opponents are using zonal marking on corner kicks, it is useful, for example, to put a player from your own team who is very good at aerial play in the zone of an opponent who is not nearly as good in that respect.

You can also organize moves that will bring one of your players who is very good at dribbling to a 1 against 1 situation after kick off or in the case of a free kick from a situation far down the field.

In figure 3 player n° 6 takes a free kick from the rear serving his teammate n° 7 who has taken up the space liberated by n° 8. Once he has received the ball, n° 7 makes for his direct opponent trying to get past him in the 1 against 1.

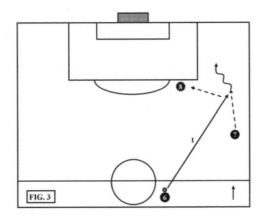

FIG. 3

Keeping possession

In particular free kick situations, the coach can train his team to opt for a choice of play that allows them to keep possession.

In cases such as the kick off, or when the keeper puts the ball back into play or in a low lying free kick you can choose a playing solution that aims to maintain possession in order to move the opponents and prepare the attacking action following your system of play and the build up of maneuvers.

Figure 4 illustrates how to keep possession following a free kick from the back: n° 6 takes the kick in favor of n° 5, who widens out the play in the direction of his teammate n° 3. He receives using the space created by n° 10's cut to enter.

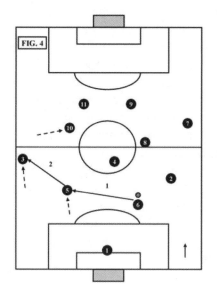

Preventive coverage and negative transition

The offensive and defensive phases are playing situations that are strictly interdependent.

Even while it is attacking, a team must be organized and well-placed for any possible loss of possession.

The mistake to be avoided is to find yourself unbalanced or slack when the opponents counterattack.

Setting the team out in preventive coverage and coaching negative transition are two things that will have to be prepared for and suitably organized. When talking about preventive coverage we are referring to the players positioned behind the line of the ball. Besides their importance in support of the offensive build up, their task is also to guarantee concrete obstruction to the opponents' play when and if the tables have been turned.

Negative transition is the switch from the attacking to the defense phase following a loss of possession.

Statistics show that an increasing number of goals are scored following so called 'breaks', that is, as the result of a fast counterattack after the opponents have lost possession.

It follows that the coach will have to train this important third phase as well as he can, adding to his training schedule exercises that aim to improve the individual and collective ability of his players in passing from the phase of possession to the phase of non-possession.

The two principles described above are crucial also as far as situations on stationary balls are concerned.

When carrying out moves on stationary balls it is necessary to include players in preventive coverage, just as the whole team must be able to get back into position once they have lost possession and not go on attacking and so running the risk of undergoing a dangerous counterattack by the opponents. In the example in Fig. 5 players nº 7, 10, 5 and 6 are in position as preventive coverage on a corner kick taken by their teammate nº 4. As we have said, these players must be ready to catch the opponents' clearances and to defend if they make a break, delaying their play to allow their own teammates to get quickly back into defense.

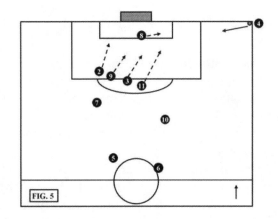

FIG. 5

CHAPTER 2

INDIVIDUAL TECHNICAL AND TACTICAL SKILLS

In this chapter we will be looking at the individual technical and tactical qualities necessary for a team to be productive in relation to set play situations in attack.

It goes without saying that, quite apart from collective organization, all those technical acts that form the play itself will need to be correctly executed for any offensive action following a free kick to be successful.

The coach must not limit himself, therefore, to training the global aspects of the play, but the group will have to receive instruction on how to carry out the following technical fundamentals:

1) Passing;
2) Oriented stopping and defending the ball;
3) Shooting on goal;
4) Heading;
5) Getting free of marking,
6) Blocking and feints
7) Dummies;
8) Dribbling

Passing

Passing can be defined as the transfer of the ball to a teammate or to a zone of the field using a suitable surface of the body.

This is without doubt the most commonly used technical act during a match.

When correctly executed this technical gesture allows the team to gain space and time during the attacking phase.

From a technical point of view we can classify passing in the following elements.

- Inside of the foot
- Inside instep
- Instep
- Outside
- Outside instep
- Heel
- Toe

The choice of what part of the foot to use in the technical act is closely connected to the distance and the ideal trajectory of the pass itself.

Depending on the distance, there are two types of pass.

- Long pass
- Short pass

The first can be carried out using the instep or the inside or outside instep. On the contrary, the other surfaces of the foot used to kick the ball - i.e., the inside, the outside, the heel and the point - are more suitable for short passes.

We can classify the trajectory of the pass in:

- A pass along the ground or in the air with a linear trajectory
- A pass along the ground or in the air that tends to bend

Having examined passes from a technical point of view, we will now take a look at the tactical aspects connected with the transfer.

Tactically speaking, the pass can be divided into:

- A pass 'onto the feet'
- A pass onto a teammate's run
- A pass into space

A pass 'onto the feet' is the transfer of the ball to a teammate who receives it on his body. A pass onto the run is when you serve the recipient as he moves to free himself of marking.
Lastly, a pass into space is used to transfer the ball in the direction of a free space which is about to be occupied by a teammate.
The pass itself may be connected to a single individual's technical skill, but, naturally, it is also a necessary part of the execution of collective attacking plays coming out of set play situations.
The coach must give continuous and effective training in all these ways of passing so the players will always be able to execute free kicks in the best way possible.

We will have to take a closer look at two particular types of passes very frequently used in dead ball situations:

+ The cross
+ The dump and rebound

The cross is a finishing touch technique that is carried out by lobbing the ball from the flank towards the center.

This type of finishing touch can be executed both with the ball in movement and in dead ball situations.

The ability to cross tightly and precisely, striking the ball principly with the inside instep of the foot on trajectories that bend in or out, or with the instep on a straight trajectory, is basic to the success of corner kicks, free kicks from the side or in developing play from a throw in.

The dump and rebound is very often used in dead ball situations and it consists of a first pass (or wall pass) executed principally by the inside of the foot (or, more rarely, by the outside or the heel) carried out in the direction of a teammate who is breaking free of marking, and it favors a shot by him or another pass.

In Fig. 6 there is an illustration of the two types of pass we have just mentioned: player nº 2 throws the ball in towards nº 9, who carries out a dump and rebound to nº 7 as he frees himself of marking. Nº 7 then crosses to the center for nº 11.

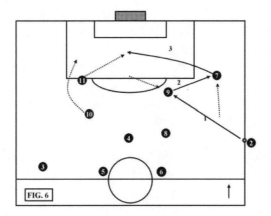

FIG. 6

The stop

The speed at which you are forced to play in modern soccer on account of teams that press all the time and who have reached very high levels of dynamic organization forces the players to move about in greatly reduced space and time.

All this has led to a change in the behavior of the player in possession and we have moved on from the 'receive, observe, decide and act' of the past, to today's 'observe, decide, receive and act'.

It therefore becomes necessary to have players ready to read the way play is developing as quickly as possible.

The different attacking plays to be used will without doubt be fundamental from the point of view of the team's organization of play, but they are based on the ability of each single player to foresee the dynamics of the attack before he gets possession of the ball.

The first thing you have to do in order to shape this ability to anticipate is to stop the ball in the best and most purposeful way.

The ball must be controlled in the technically correct way; and this must be done purposefully, in the sense that it must be 'oriented', i.e., carried out in a direction that is the most suitable to the situation of play.

In connection with this last aspect, it is important to underline the position of the body assumed by the recipient.

In fact, having first read the situation of play with care, weighing up the position of the ball, of his teammates and his opponents, he will then have to place himself in the most functional manner for any future pass he is to carry out.

For example, if he decides to pass to his left with an opponent arriving from his right, he will have to place his body facing the chosen direction so as to make it easier to carry out the pass and, at the same time, to protect himself from his opponent's intervention.

In cases where he receives the pass with an opponent marking him tightly, he will have to protect the ball with his body and carry out a backward dump.

Fluid and constant attacking maneuvers are the most important objectives to be reached in an effective attacking phase, but you will only be able to carry them out if you have players who, unable to use one touch exchanges, will be able to control their teammates' passes successfully, thus allowing their team to build up speed.

In order to distinguish the various types of reception, we can make a first classification on the basis of the surfaces of the body involved:

+ Inside of the foot
+ Outside of the foot
+ Instep
+ Sole
+ Thigh
+ Stomach
+ Chest
+ Head

Another classification can be made referring to the way in which it is carried out:

+ With the ball on the ground
+ Drop stop (counter bounce)
+ With the ball in flight
+ On a tight or parabolic trajectory

From all this it will be clear that good, purposeful execution of the stop in all its variants is crucial even when you are organizing attacking situations with set plays.

Shooting on goal

The shot on goal is the conclusive act to an action in attack.
In consideration of its particular objective, the shot on goal will need to have two essential prerequisites:

+ Precision, when at a minimal distance from the goal and the ball must only be directed with accuracy.
+ Power, when there is a great distance from the goal and you need the maximum drive to cover that gap.

The shot can be carried out in two principle ways:

* With your foot
* With your head

In this paragraph we will be looking at shots using the feet, leaving the second type to the section relative to heading the ball.
Shots using the feet can be divided into a great number of technical solutions.
They can be carried out by:

* The instep
* The outside instep
* The inside instep
* The inside
* The outside
* The toe
* The heel

We have put shots using the toe on the list because this way of kicking the ball - which does not involve much force on the part of the body - can often be useful in resolving crowded situations in the area or beating the defender or the keeper to the ball.
The player taking the shot can find himself in the following situations in relation to the opponents:

* Without opposition
* With an opponent in front
* With an opponent to his side
* With an opponent behind him who is just realizing what is about to happen

Having made a short but necessary run-down of the shot itself, we will now have a look at the specifics to vary to be able to organize a series of exercises aimed at giving global training in shooting on goal.

The best exercises the coach can do are those that vary:
- The part of the foot that carries out the shot;
- The distance of the player shooting from the goal with consequent placement of the keeper:
  - Outside the area
  - From the limit of the area
  - With the keeper coming out
  - Inside the area
  - After a bounce

- The defender's pressure on the player taking the kick:
  - With the defender in front of or beside the striker
  - With the defender trying to recover ground
  - Without any immediate opposition

It goes without saying that this technical act - so important because of its final objective - will have to be coached in all its variations, and good coaching will be decisive in the success of all dead ball situations carried out to set up shots on goal.

Heading the ball

Another fundamental skill in soccer is the ability to use your head in attacking or defensive situations of play.
The head is second only to the feet as the most frequently used part of the body in a match. Players use their heads in attack for the following reasons:

- To pass
- To shoot on goal
- To prolong (flick on)
- To rebound (dump and rebound)

As far as actually carrying out the act is concerned, you can execute the header:

- With your feet on the ground
- Jumping straight into the air (two foot jump)
- Jumping after a run up (one foot jump)
- Diving

The best parts of the head for striking the ball are the following:

- The upper forehead
- The lower forehead
- The sides of the head

We must have a closer look now at a particular type of header: the prolonging pass(flick on). This consists of hitting the ball with the upper part of the forehead in order to lengthen its trajectory.

Fig. 7 shows a play foreseeing the use of the prolonging header: player n° 6 takes a free kick near the half way line, kicking it deep towards n° 9 who prolongs to n° 11 as he breaks in, and n° 11 shoots.

As we have just seen, the header is frequently used even on set plays, both to shoot on goal and to carry out dump and rebounds and prolonging passes.

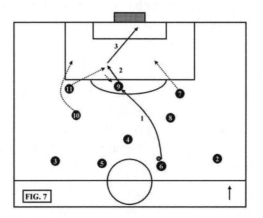

FIG. 7

Good coaching in connection with the various types of headers and their variations is necessary in order to make set plays as dangerous and effective as possible.

Breaking free of marking

Breaking free of marking is a vital principle of individual tactics during the attacking phase. The ability to get free of marking and occupy a free space (a part of the field not engaged by opponents or teammates) must be considered a central skill of each player involved in the attack, setting up good passing solutions for teammates in possession and making it possible to build up fast fluid and cohesive attacking play.

This skill is also fundamental in making the best of dead ball situations.

The single player's movements without the ball will have to be organized into movements of the team in order to satisfy one of the most important attacking principles in collective tactics which we have already discussed: mobility.

The most important thing is to respect the two fundamental specifics of the game of soccer (space and time), and so, in reaction to every movement on the field, the players will have to keep to the following needs:

a) Why?

As we have already said, it is essential to move without the ball in order to offer good passing opportunities to your teammate in possession.

When you get free of marking you are aiming at two things: the aggressive occupation of a free space on the one hand; and the consequent creation of a space that can be attacked by a teammate on the other. The whole series of players' movements to occupy and liberate spaces, if they are carried out in a well-organized context and timed in relation to the kick taken by the player putting the ball back into play, will allow the team to develop effective set plays (cf. Fig. 1).

b) Where?

If it is to be achieved in a well-organized set play, the act of breaking free of marking will frequently have to be carried out in a pre-established space.

Generally speaking the recipient's movement without the ball must be made into the 'zone of light', i.e., into a space that is visible to the player in possession and which can therefore be reached by the pass itself.

It is, lastly, of the utmost importance that the possible recipient comes out of the opponent's 'shadow cone' without letting himself be covered and avoiding the risk of remaining outside play on account of the clear possibility of the pass being intercepted.

c) How?

A player moving to free himself of marking will have to do so by running diagonally. The diagonal sprint is the best way to effectively break out of marking because of the number of advantages it will bring, specifically:

- It allows the player without the ball to see the teammate who is about to pass to him (and therefore also the ball), the goal and the defender who is marking him.
- Being able to see the player carrying out the pass is very important because it allows you to time the play, as we will see later when we talk about 'when' to break free of marking.
- It makes it much more difficult for the opponents to anticipate because the recipient will have more chance to put his body between the ball and the defender.
- The pass will have to be carried out by the foot that is further away from the opponent if he is near the recipient. If the marker has not followed the movement to break free of his marking, the pass should be carried out with the inside foot to put the attacking player in a position to turn around more quickly.
- It increases the angles of the passes, widening out the playing spaces. Having more space will of course simplify the execution of the pass and create greater flow in the build up.

In cases where the player without the ball is being tightly marked by an opponent (and this is the most frequent situation), then his break to free himself can be divided into two strictly connected movements. The first is a move to trick his opponent, often called a 'countermovement' in which the attacking player usually moves in the opposite direction from the space that he really intends to attack. It is then followed by the real move to free himself of marking, carried out by a sudden change of direction and speed, going in the opposite way from the countermovement he goes to take up position in the space in which he has decided to receive the pass. In some cases, when the attacking player is too far away from the zone of reception, his move to free himself of marking can be accompanied by a preparatory movement, which can be called an 'approach', and whose aim is to get nearer to the space he intends to attack.

As we can see in Fig. 8, player nº 8 breaks in along the flank with a diagonal run after having made a countermovement pretending to go to meet the ball and then occupying the space left free by nº 7.

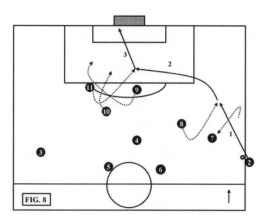

d) When?

As we said in the first chapter, conventional signs are very often agreed on (e.g., raising or lowering an arm), or specific technical acts (e.g., a player touches the ball to a teammate, who stops it with the sole of his boot) can be used both to synchronize the moves and to give the recipient time to attack space as well as he can (cf. Fig. 1).

Blocks and veils

Blocks and veils are actions whose aim it is to set up a teammate's move to break away while at the same time obstructing the opposing defender trying to mark him.

That is to say, these movements tend to interrupt the continuity with which an opponent is marking a teammate.

Both blocks and veils are widely used in set plays to free a teammate to shoot or use finishing touches. The difference between them is that blocks are used by the player in a static way while veils are more dynamic.

We should add that in soccer the block can be punished as a foul of obstruction, and should therefore be carried out quickly and with care.

In order to distinguish between these actions of disturbance on the opponent, it is better to use the veil rather than the block for two reasons.

    a) The veil is always permitted;
    b) The player who carries it out is in movement and so has a
       more active role in the attacking phase.

We must point out, however, that the block has the advantage of being a greater obstacle for the opponent to get past, and is easier to carry out. As it is a very dynamic action, the veil requires great timing and synchronism of movement.

The differences can be seen in Figs. 9 and 10.

In fig. 9, player n° 8 takes the free kick from the side, serving teammate n° 9, who shoots using a block by n° 10 on his own opponent.

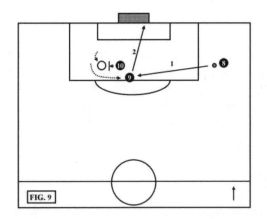

FIG. 9

In fig. 10, n° 8 takes a corner sending the ball to the far post in the direction of n° 9, who had freed himself of marking by using teammate n° 6's veil.

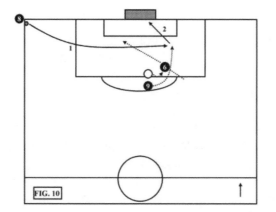

FIG. 10

The dummy

In this context what we mean by dummy is a misleading movement by a player who goes to meet the ball, 'pretending' to intervene, but letting it pass to another teammate.

This type of action is frequently used in dead ball situations, mainly on corners or free kicks, with the intention of freeing a player to shoot or set up finishing touches.

In Fig. 11 we can see a situation in which a dummy leads to a situation from which it is possible to shoot: player nº 8 takes a corner kick along the ground to nº 9, who has gone to meet the ball.

Nº 9 carries out a dummy in favor of nº 10, who shoots on goal.

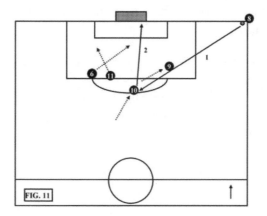

FIG. 11

Dribbling

Dribbling is the ability to get past an opponent with the ball.
It is an individual technical and tactical play which has very important effects even on collective tactics.
Dribbling past an opponent will give two main advantages:

- An open ball, with the resultant opportunity of carrying out a vertical pass without opposition from the opponents,
- Numerical superiority, which will force the opposing team to carry out shifting movements that can destabilize their organization if they are not done by heart and with the correct timing.

A player who can get past an opponent with a dribble automatically creates free space and momentarily excludes an opponent from the play.
It is very useful for a team to have players capable of carrying out this type of play because in themselves they create space and they also disorient the opponents. Dribbling must never be done as a thing in itself, but must always help to develop good attacking play. Guiding the ball in order to dribble past an opponent is done in order to.

- Create space in front
- Shoot
- Pass and cross
- Get over the opponents pressure, making their pressing ineffective

This particular ability is necessary in order to make the best of play on stationary balls.
When the ball is put back into play, certain attacking solutions can immediately create 1 against 1 situations in which a player is encouraged to dribble past his opponent (cf. Fig. 3).

CHAPTER 3

AN ANALYSIS OF
DEAD BALL SITUATIONS

Having examined the general principles and the individual technical and tactical qualities needed to make the best of set plays, we will now go on to have a more specific look at the single types of situations in connection.

We will start off with an analysis of the situations following the kick off and then develop the study by considering the keeper putting the ball back into play, free kicks, corners and throw ins.

Kick off

The resumption of play must be organized like any of the other dead ball situations that take place more frequently during a match.

You can structure attacking movements at the kick off by following two main strategies of play:

- Possession play aiming to prepare your build up and finishing touch plays, trying to move the opponents into a pre-defined zone of the field.
- Immediate vertical play trying to take control of space, to widen out the front of the attack and get into a situation that will be favorable for the 1 against 1.

If you decide to go for this second playing solution, you will need to have a man on the team who has a long and precise kick, a teammate good at aerial play and one who is good at dribbling and crossing.

Kick off n° 1 (Fig. 12)

Players n° 4 and n° 9 take the kick off touching backwards to n° 8, who launches along the flanks towards n° 10.

N° 10 lengthens out the trajectory, flicking with his head towards n° 7, who, once he has controlled the pass, has two solutions open to him for the cross: n° 9 on the near post and n° 11 on the far post.

N° 3's job is to give support to n° 10 in case there is a back rebound or a clearance by the opponents.

In this example 7's cross favors n° 11's shot on goal.

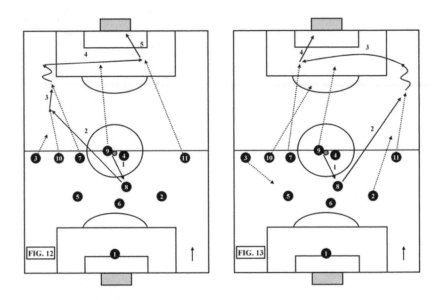

Kick off nº 2 (Fig. 13)

Players nº 4 and nº 9 take the kick off, touching back to nº 8, who fakes a pass along the left flank where there are three teammates, but instead makes a long pass to nº 11 who has broken in on the right flank.

Once he has controlled the pass, nº 11 will try to get past his direct opponent in the 1 against 1 in order to go for a cross to his teammates in the center who have followed the action. In this example, nº 11's cross favors his teammate nº 7's shot on goal, where he has attacked the space on the far post. Nº 2's movement is important, shortening up in nº 11's direction in order to give support and to act as preventive coverage.

On the weak side nº 3 tightens in to the center to make the defense section more compact.

Kick off nº 3 (Fig. 14)

Players nº 4 and nº 9 take the kick off, touching back to nº 8, who makes a long pass along the right flank in the direction of 11who is breaking in.

Nº 11 makes a wall pass back towards supporting player nº 10, who changes play towards nº 3 who is breaking away on the left.

Nº 3 has three solutions for the cross.
In the example, the cross in favor of nº 9, who shoots from the center of the area.

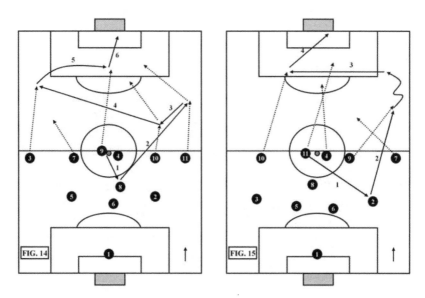

Kick off nº 4 (Fig. 15)

Players nº 11 and 4 take the kick off, making a diagonal back pass to nº 2. He makes a long pass up the flank for nº 9, who has broken in to the right, crossing over with nº 7.
Nº 9 opts for a personal solution, dribbling past his direct opponent and crossing to nº 10, who has attacked space on the second post.

Kick off nº 5 (Fig. 16)

Players nº 11 and 4 take the kick off, making a diagonal back pass to nº 2; he kicks long to nº 9, who has broken in. Nº 9 flicks the ball to nº 4, who shoots.

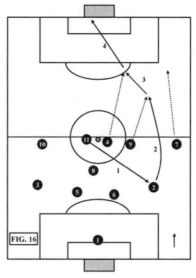

The keeper puts the ball back into play

In this dead ball situation it is very important to have a keeper good at playing with his feet on both short and long passes.

The 'Number One' will have to do special training in these specific plays.

It is not a good idea to get a mobile player to kick the ball back into play from the base line because that will lengthen out the team, conceding wide open spaces to the opponents, with the negative consequences that are easy to imagine. The most frequently used solution in this situation is the long clearance by the keeper, preferably to an area of the field controlled by a teammate good at aerial play.

This type of solution is not very productive because you have only a 50% chance of getting possession of the ball. In line with the ideas set out in this book, it is unadvisable to choose this type of solution for the very reason it is not really possible to organize it in an effective way. Instead, there are two main strategic choices that are to be considered better:

- ◆ Short play by the keeper to the area of the field less densely occupied by the opponents, with his own team widening out to receive it. After the initial pass the building up movements will have to be organized in the way most suitable to the characteristics of the team, considering the dangerous zone from which the play has started off (Fig. 17).
- ◆ Arranging organized movements to create and occupy spaces in consideration of the players' characteristics.

The keeper puts the ball back into play, N° 1 (Fig. 18)

The keeper kicks the clearance in the direction of n° 9, who uses the space created by n° 8 breaking into space in depth. N° 9 has three solutions for his deviation: side players n° 11 and 7's cuts and 8's breaking in towards the center. In this case the deviation favors n° 8's breaking free of marking, and he shoots.

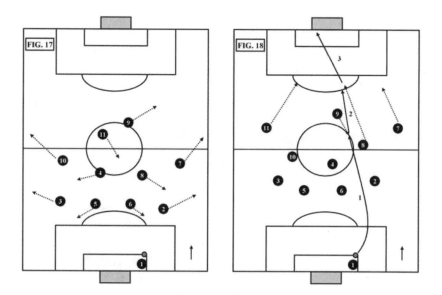

The keeper puts the ball back into play, N° 2 (Fig. 19)

The keeper kicks along the flanks towards n° 8, who has crossed over with his teammate n° 7. N° 8 dumps on n° 2, who has gone to support, and he can now build up an attacking action facing the goal.

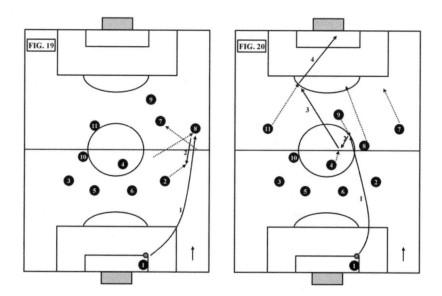

The keeper puts the ball back into play, N° 3 (Fig. 20)

The keeper clears towards n° 9, who uses the space created by n° 8 as he breaks in at the front.
N° 9 dumps on n° 4 who has come up in support. He now has three passing solutions: the side cuts of n° 11 and 7, and n° 8 breaking into the center.
In this example, n° 4 passes to n° 11, who shoots.

Free kicks

The free kick is one of the most frequent dead ball situations in matches.
The different positions from which it is possible to take a free kick (practically from all over the playing field) allow you to structure a great number of plays, which must be organized so that you can exploit the characteristics of your players.
Free kick situations can be classified in two main ways:

- Direct free kick
- Indirect free kick

The first solution allows you to shoot directly on goal.
It is very important to have specialists in the team who are good at shooting directly on goal.
Keeping in mind the distance from the goal, shooting directly from a free kick can be carried out using:

- The inside or outside instep, which allows you to bend the trajectory as well as giving fairly good power (this is the most usual choice).
- The instep, which gives you a straight trajectory but with excellent power.

To make the best possible use of a direct free kick, it is also important to use other players in support of the one who is actually kicking.
When shooting from close to the limits of the penalty area, it is a good idea to put at least two players beside the last player in the wall to disturb the keeper's vision.

Another player can be placed beside the kicker and he can dummy the shot (for example, passing over the ball) to make the opponents unsure about what type of playing solution will actually be used.

Fig. 21 illustrates an organized situation on a direct free kick: player n° 7 passes over the ball, feinting the kick and so favors n° 9's shot.

After the shot, teammates n° 9 and 10, initially placed on the wall, will go towards the goal 'hunting' for the possible rebound.

N° 3 and 6 will also be looking for such a chance.

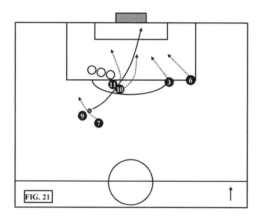

FIG. 21

Indirect free kick situations also give a great variety of solutions, which, as we have already said, must try to exploit the skills of the players.

We will now illustrate many plays that can be used, and which are to be considered and selected in connection with your particular needs.

We will be considering free kick situations from the sides first of all,.

The plays proposed illustrate solutions with crosses to the center and moves that will allow for central shots using dump and rebounds and combinations. As we have already said, when crossing to the center it is important to give training on the synchronization between the actual kick and the movements of the players who are receiving.

When crossing, you can use trajectories going in or coming out. Theoretically, the first are principally used for solutions on the second post, and the second for those nearer to the player taking the kick.

In the second place, we will be looking at plays relative to indirect free kicks from a central position, and, lastly, three solutions for how to restart play on free kicks taken from the defensive half of the field.

Side free kick N° 1 (Fig. 22)

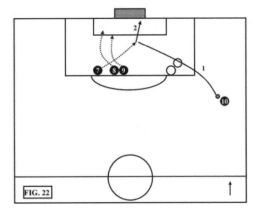

Side free kick from an in depth position: player 10 kicks tight on the near post with a trajectory coming out. Numbers 8 and 9 carry out a movement towards the far post, so freeing space on the near post. Player 7 uses 8 and 9's veiling movements, attacking the near post and shooting. He can head or kick the ball on the run.

Side free kick N° 2 (Fig. 23)

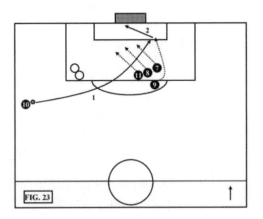

Player n° 10 takes this in-depth side free kick, sending the ball onto the far post with an in-swinging trajectory. Numbers 11, 8 and 7, positioned on the far post, cut towards the near post, freeing space.

Player n° 9 carries out a semi circular movement using 7's veil and attacking the space freed by his teammates on the far post to receive 10's cross. 9 can head or kick the ball on the run.

Side free kick N° 3 (Fig. 24)

Player n° 10 takes an in-depth side free kick, sending the ball to n° 11, who goes to meet it using 9's block and his teammates' movement towards the goal. It is important that 7 and 8's movement is carried out so as to free the near post, making sure that 11's shot does not rebound off his teammates. The two players who are creating space must also be careful not to finish up in an offside position. It is advisable as well that 10 should pass along the ground to 11 so that he can shoot directly on goal.

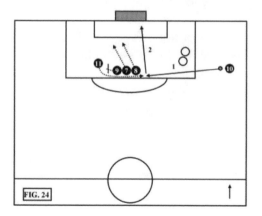

FIG. 24

Side free kick N° 4 (Fig. 25)

Player n° 8 kicks an in-depth free kick towards n° 9, who has gone to meet the ball using n° 7's block.

N° 9 carries out a feint, after which he moves in a semi-circle to receive 10's rebound into the area. He then shoots on goal.

N° 11 attacks the space on the far post in case the trajectory of the shot is off the goal, or because his teammate might decide to cross to the center if he finds himself too much to the side.

It is best in this play if all the passes are tight and along the ground.

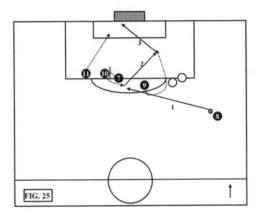

Side free kick N° 5 (Fig. 26)

This is a variant of the preceding play.
Player n° 8 takes the side free kick, sending the ball to n° 11, who has gone to meet it using n° 10's block.
N° 11 dumps on 9, who, initially placed in front of the wall, has broken free of marking in the area.
N° 7 attacks space in front on the far post in case the trajectory of the shot is off the goal, or because his teammate might decide to cross to the center if he finds himself too much to the side.
It is important that the player who is going to shoot starts off just after 8 kicks so the timing is right for 11's rebound.
This play can also be carried out in a more central position.
The passes must be tight and along the ground.

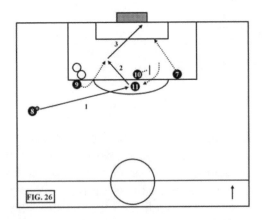

Side free kick N° 6 (Fig. 27)

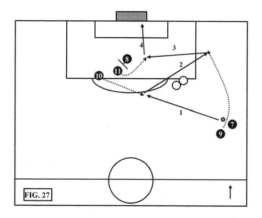

Player n° 9 passes over the ball, breaking in along the flank.
His teammate n° 7 takes the free kick towards 10, who has come to meet the ball.
He rebounds on n° 9, who has broken in.
Having received the ball, n° 9 carries out a cross on the near post in favor of 11, who has used his teammate n° 8's block.
It is very important to time this play correctly, above all as concerns the movements of the players inside the penalty area.

Side free kick N° 7 (Fig. 28)

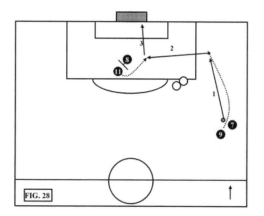

This is a similar play to the last.

Player n° 9 passes over the ball, breaking in along the flank.

His teammate n° 7 takes the free kick towards n° 9, who has broken in.

Having received the ball, player n° 9 crosses on the near post in favor of 11, who has used his teammate n° 8's block.

It is very important to time this play correctly, above all as concerns the movements of the players inside the penalty area.

Side free kick N° 8 (Fig. 29)

Initially placed in front of the last man in the wall, player n° 11 then gets free of marking into depth above the wall itself and break in along the flank. N° 10 takes the free kick, serving his teammate n° 11's run as he widens out. When he has received the ball, n° 11 crosses onto the far post to 9, who has used n° 7's block. It is important that n° 10 times his pass on the basis of 11's movement, which is what sets off the play.

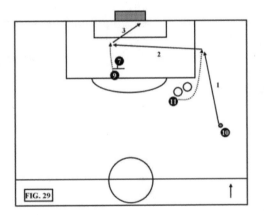

FIG. 29

Side free kick N° 9 (Fig. 30)

The free kick is taken by n° 10, who kicks a tight ball to the center with its trajectory circling outwards in the direction of teammate n° 8, who attacks space created by the widening out movements of 9 and 11.

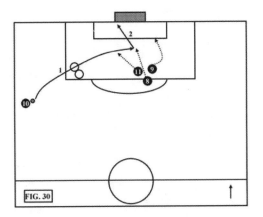

Side free kick n° 10 (Fig. 31)

Player n° 8 takes the side free kick, sending it with an out-swinging trajectory on the far post, where n° 9 has freed himself using his teammate n° 10's block. N° 9 carries out a rebound with his head for 11, who has freed himself of marking in the center using his teammate n° 7's block.
N° 11 makes a first touch shot on goal.

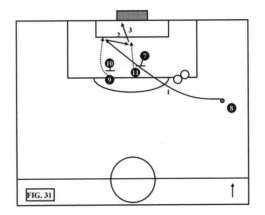

Side free kick n° 11 (Fig. 32)

Player n° 11 takes the side free kick, touching to 9, who stops the ball with his sole first of all, then passes to his teammate n° 4, who has broken into the central space freed by 10 and 8's widening out movements.
As soon as n° 4 gets to the ball he shoots on goal.

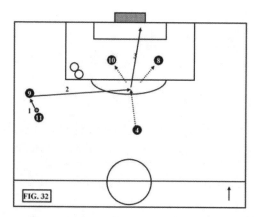

Side free kick n° 12 (Fig. 33)

Player n° 7 takes the side free kick from near the base line and he gives it an out-swinging trajectory.
The three players n° 9, 8 and 5 carry out a movement backwards to create free space near the goal.
N° 10, 11 and 6 attack the space left free by the backward movement of their teammates and they go to the center and on the near and far post.
N° 7 then has three solutions open to him when he takes the free kick.
In this example n° 7 serves 10 on the near post.
Teammates n° 9, 8 and 5 must be ready to attack any possible clearances.

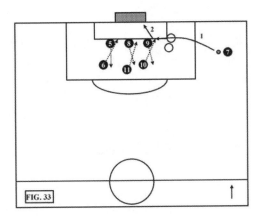

Side free kick N° 13 (Fig. 34)

Player n° 7 takes the free kick with an in-swinging trajectory.
The four teammates in the center carry out a diagonal movement into depth towards the goal.
The in-swinging cross puts the opponents' keeper in difficulty, and a little deviation will be enough to get past him.
In this example it is n° 9 who shoots.
The in depth movements of the players in the center of the area can also work as feints in cases where the cross is aimed directly at the goal.

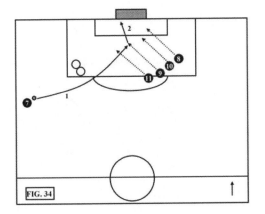

Side free kick N° 14 (Fig. 35)

The three players 10, 8 and 9 are on the ball to take a free kick from the side. N° 10 touches to 8, who controls the ball with his sole, apparently to give n° 9 a chance to shoot.
When 9 is just about to get to the ball, n° 8 touches backwards with his heel or sole to n° 4, who is running up, and 4 shoots at goal.
Players n° 11 and 7 cut towards the goal in case of a rebound or to deviate the trajectory of the shot itself.

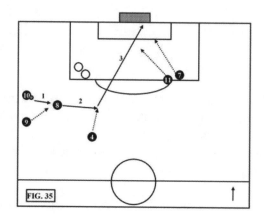

Side free kick N° 15 (Fig. 36)

Player n° 10 takes a side free kick along the ground towards 9, who has gone to meet the ball from the center of the area.

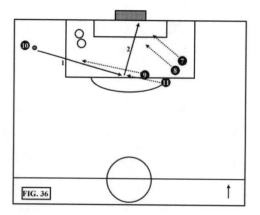

48

N° 9 feints to the advantage of n° 11, who shoots.

The best thing, naturally, is for a left-footed player to take the free kick from the left and a right-footed one from the right.

Players n° 8 and 7 cut towards the goal in case of a rebound or to deviate the trajectory of the shot itself.

Side free kick N° 16 (Fig. 37)

Player n° 8 takes a side free kick towards 9, who has come to meet the ball.

When 9 has received the pass, he rebounds backwards to n° 4, who is running up and 4 shoots at goal.

Players n° 8 and 10 cut towards the goal in case of a rebound or to deviate the trajectory of the shot itself.

It is best if the players pass along the ground, making sure that they are accurate.

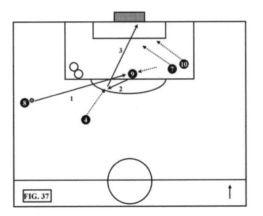

FIG. 37

Side free kick N° 17 (Fig. 38)

Player n° 4 takes a side free kick on the near post with an out-swinging trajectory towards n° 8. 8 then flicks on with his head to 9, who has gone to take up position on the far post.

Player n° 9 uses his teammate n° 11's block in the area.

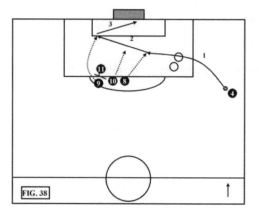

FIG. 38

Side free kick N° 18 (Fig. 39)

Player n° 8 takes a side free kick in the attacking zone, sending the ball tight with an out-swinging trajectory on the near post towards n° 7, who has used his teammate n° 10's block. Players n° 11 and 9 attack space on the far post in the center in case 8's cross goes over n° 7's head.

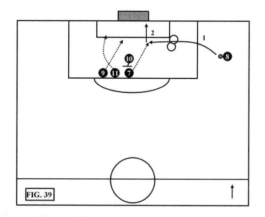

FIG. 39

Side free kick N° 19 (Fig. 40)

Player n° 8 takes a side free kick in the attacking zone, sending the ball tight with an in-swinging trajectory on the far post towards n° 11, who has used his teammate n° 7's block. Players n° 10 and 9 attack space on the far post in the center in case 8's cross goes short.

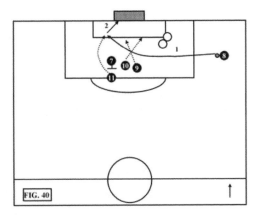

Side free kick N° 20 (Fig. 41)

Player n° 7 takes a side free kick in the attacking zone. The four players in the center group themselves close together. Player n° 9 uses 8's veil and attacks space on the near post, while n° 6 uses 4's veil and occupies the far post. In this example the free kick is sent to the far post with an in-swinging trajectory towards n° 6, who then shoots.

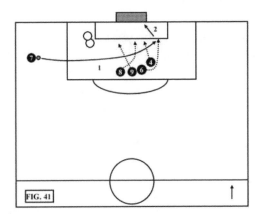

Side free kick N° 21 (Fig. 42)

The side free kick is taken by player n° 10, who sends the ball tight and along the ground towards the far post into the space created by the three players 9, 11 and 7, who cut in pretending to receive the cross.
Instead, the pass is sent to n° 2, who shoots from the edge of the area.

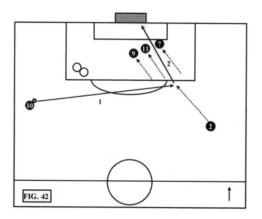

Side free kick N° 22 (Fig. 43)

The side free kick is taken by player n° 7 towards 9, who has come to meet the ball. N° 9 dummies in favor of 11, who passes to his teammate n° 10 who has freed himself of marking in the area.
Player n° 8 cuts towards the far post in case of a rebound or to deviate the trajectory of the shot itself.

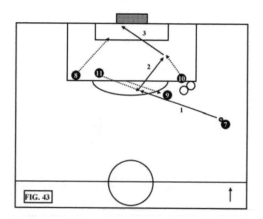

Side free kick N° 23 (Fig. 44)

Player n° 6 takes the side free kick from an in-depth position, serving n° 4 at the edge of the area in line with the far post and in the space created by 7 and 8's cuts.
The two teammates n° 9 and n° 10, positioned on the near post, make a movement to come out, placing themselves in coverage on 4 (in case he is either anticipated by an opponent or his shot is cleared).

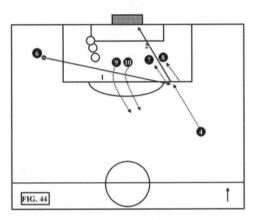

Side free kick N° 24 (Fig. 45)

Player n° 2 takes a side free kick towards 9 from near the half way line. N° 9 passes to his teammate n° 7, who has come to meet the ball and then freed himself of marking along the flank.
N° 7 crosses to the far post to teammate n° 11, who has exploited n° 10's block.

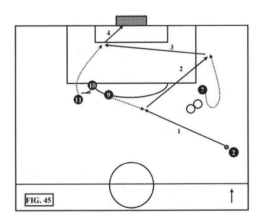

Central free kick N° 1 (Fig. 46)

Player n° 8 passes over the ball, breaking into the penalty area. Teammate n° 7 passes along the ground for n° 9, who has gone to meet the ball. N° 9 then passes to 8 as he breaks in, and 8 shoots at goal.
Player n° 11 cuts towards the far post in case of a rebound or to deviate the trajectory of the shot itself.

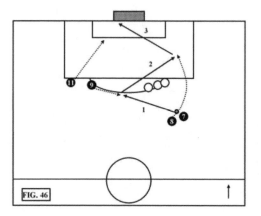

Central free kick N° 2 (Fig. 47)

Player n° 8 feints a side pass for 4's shot, and instead sends a bender over the heads of the wall for 7 as he breaks in, and 7 shoots.
It is important for 7 to time his move to break free of marking with care so that he does not end up in an offside position.

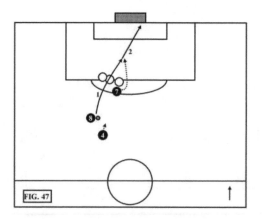

Central free kick N° 3 (Fig. 48)

Player n° 4 takes the free kick, bending the ball towards 7's move to break free of marking into the space created by 11 and 9's cuts. When n° 7 arrives on the ball he can shoot at once if he is sufficiently free, or he can pass to his teammates in the area, who must, of course, follow the action.

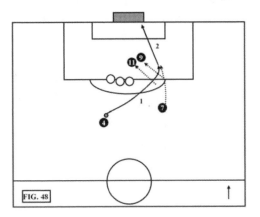

Central free kick N° 4 (Fig. 49)

Player n° 10 feints a side pass for n° 6's shot, but sends the ball instead towards the center, curving it over the wall towards n° 9, who has broken in using 7's block.
Player n° 9 must be careful not to get caught offside.

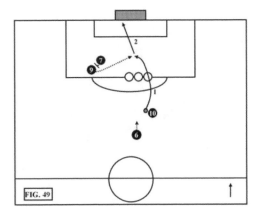

Central free kick N° 5 (Fig. 50)

Player n° 4 takes a central free kick from downfield towards the far post for n° 9. N° 9 passes with his head to one of his teammates who has freed himself of marking in the area.: 7 and 11 attack the space in front of the goal, n° 11 gets free of marking behind n° 9, while n° 8 shortens in on any possible clearance by the opponents. In this example the ball goes to player n° 7. Naturally, this scheme can only be used if you have a player who is very good in the air.

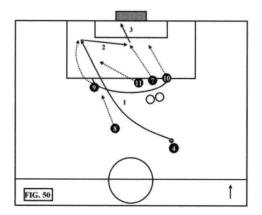

Central free kick N° 6 (Fig. 51)

Player n° 4 takes a free kick making a side pass towards n° 7. N° 7 then crosses to the far post with an in-swinging trajectory towards n° 11, who has freed himself of marking using 9's block.
It is a good idea for n° 7 to be left-footed if positioned on the right, and right-footed if on the other side.

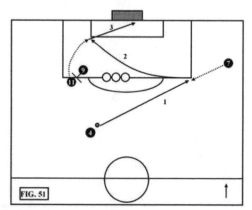

Central free kick N° 7 (Fig. 52)

Player n° 6 takes a central free kick, feinting a cross to the center, and instead making a side pass to teammate n° 11, who returns the ball to him.
N° 6 now serves n° 3, who has overlapped 11, breaking in along the flank.
When he has arrived to 6's pass, player n° 3 crosses to the near post towards n° 9, who has used 8's block.

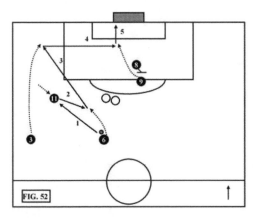

Central free kick N° 8 (Fig. 53)

Player n° 6 is on the ball; he feints a side pass for 4's shot, but then serves n° 9, placed in front of the wall.
N° 9 passes to n° 7 as he runs up, and 7 shoots on goal.

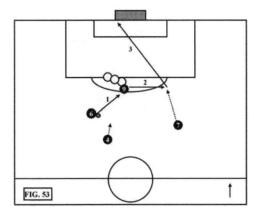

Central free kick N° 9 (Fig. 54)

The central free kick is taken by player n° 8, who feints a touch for 6's shot, but then serves teammate n° 10, initially placed in front of the wall but then moving to break free of marking.
When 8's pass arrives to him, n° 10 shoots.
It is best to put a left-footed player in the wall if he is getting free of marking to the left and a right-footed one to the right.

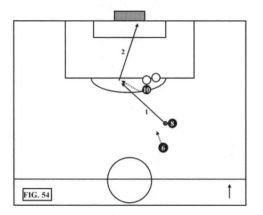

Central free kick N° 10 (Fig. 55)

Player n° 10 is on the ball and pretends to take the free kick in favor of his teammate n° 8, placed in such a way as to stop the ball for 4's shot.
Instead, n° 10 passes to n° 9 positioned in front of the wall; 9 passes to n° 8, who shoots after he has freed himself of marking to the side.

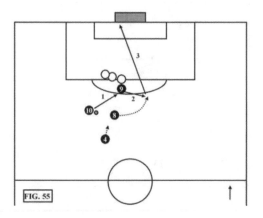

Free kick in the defensive half, N° 1 (Fig. 56)

This play can be made if you have a player good at aerial play and one who has a long and precise kick.

The free kick is taken by n° 5, who sends the ball long in the direction of n° 9 from his own half. N° 9 flicks the ball on with three teammates (7, 10 and 11) attacking space in depth in order to receive 9's head pass. The two players 4 and 8 shorten up on 9 to give him support for his rebound and to get possession of the opponents' clearance.

In this way, n° 9 has 5 passing solutions: in this example, n° 11 gets the pass and shoots.

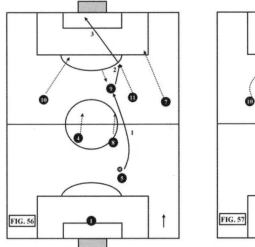
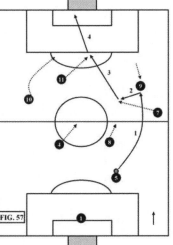

Free kick in the defensive half, N° 2 (Fig. 57)

This play can be made if you have a player good at aerial play and one who has a long and precise kick.

The free kick is taken in his own half by n° 5, who kicks long towards 9 as he comes to meet the ball. N° 9 then passes with his head to n° 7, who has cut in towards the center.

The two mid fielders 4 and 8 shorten in to intercept a possible clearance or to give support to 9 and 7, but they must be careful not to bring opponents into the space where 7 has to receive the ball.

N° 7 can serve either n° 10 or n° 11.

In this example the assist goes to 11, who shoots.

Free kick in the defensive half, N° 3 (Fig. 58)

This play can be carried out if you do not have a striker good at aerial play. Player n° 6 takes the free kick from his own defensive half, sending a long pass up the flanks to n° 9 as he widens out and crosses over with n° 7. N° 9 passes back to n° 8 as he runs up in support, and he serves teammate n° 11, who shoots after cutting in.

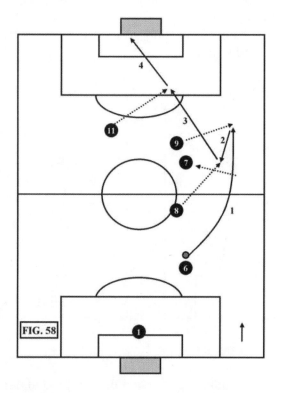

The corner kick

The corner is a common dead ball situation in every match. In line with all that has already been said, you must train for this situation with great attention and care so that your team reaches a good level of organization on these kinds of stationary balls. Once again, it is very important to have players good at kicking corners, who can cross to the center with good precision and suitable force (as far as the trajectories are concerned -i.e., out or in-swinging - what we have said about free kicks is in force here as well).

In the same way, it is vital to synchronize the timing of the kick with the receiver's movements without the ball.

In connection with the receiving players, their ability in aerial play and in making one touch shots will of course be decisive factors.

We will now be illustrating a great number of plays that tend to put the aerial skills of your players on show, without at the same time neglecting low ball solutions and combinations, in cases where you do not have players with real aerial ability.

Plays

Corner kick N° 1 (Fig. 59)

Player n° 10 takes the corner, passing back to n° 8 as he runs up. He crosses to the far post, with an out-swinging trajectory in the direction of teammate n° 9, who is making use of 5's block.

N° 6 and n° 11 attack respectively the near post and the center in case the cross falls short.

Having carried out the block, n° 5 must be ready to intercept any possible clearances in the area.

N° 7 goes up to occupy space outside the area so that he can catch any clearances and to give preventive coverage.

It is best if n° 8 is right-footed for corners taken from the right and left footed for those from the left.

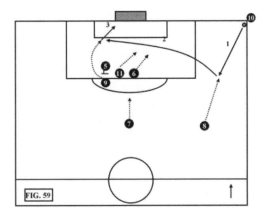

FIG. 59

Corner kick N° 2 (Fig. 60)

The corner is taken by n° 10 who kicks along the ground towards 8, who comes to meet the ball.
As soon as he gets near the ball, n° 8 dummies to the advantage of teammate n° 11, who shoots.
The two teammates, 5 and 9, attack respectively the far and the near post to free space in the center for 11's shot, and they must be ready to pounce on the rebound or to deflect the shot.
N° 6 moves backwards to give coverage to n° 11 in case he is anticipated or his shot is cleared.

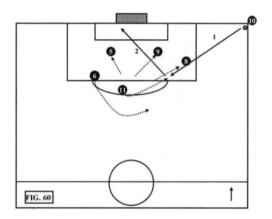

Corner kick N° 3 (Fig. 61)

The corner is taken by n° 10, serving n° 8 as he runs up.
Having kicked the ball, n° 10 overlaps 8, receiving his return pass. Then player n° 10 makes an in-swinging cross to the far post towards 11, who has freed himself of marking using 6's veil into depth. With n° 6, teammates 9 and 5 cut onto the near post and to the center, freeing space on the far post.
N° 7 occupies space outside the area to gather the clearances and to give preventive coverage.

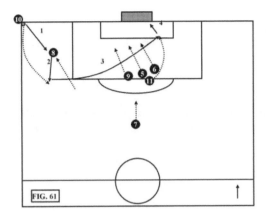

FIG. 61

Corner kick N° 4 (Fig. 62)

This play requires the corner to be kicked with an in-swinging trajectory.
From the right a left-footed player needs to kick and a right-footed one from the opposite side.
In this example the corner is taken by n° 10 with an in-swinging trajectory to the near post towards n° 9, who flicks onto the far post for n° 5 as he attacks that space making use of his teammate n° 11's block. N° 6 and n° 8 go into the space behind n° 9 in case 10's cross goes over the center forward's head.
After having made the block, player n° 11 must be ready to pounce on any possible clearances in the area. N° 7 goes to occupy space outside the area to gather the clearances and give preventive coverage.

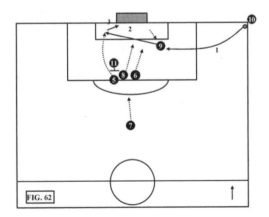

FIG. 62

Corner kick N° 5 (Fig. 63)

Also in this play it is best to use an in-swinging trajectory.
Player n° 10 takes the corner, kicking onto the far post.
Teammates 5, 11 and 8 cut onto the near post and to the center,
creating space on the far post.
Player n° 9 attacks the far post with a semi circular movement,
making use of his teammate n° 8's veil run, and then shoots.
N° 7 goes up to occupy space outside the area to gather any
clearances and give preventive coverage.

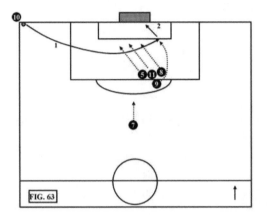

Corner kick N° 6 (Fig 64)

Player n° 10 takes the corner, kicking tight on the near post with an
out-swinging trajectory. Here, n° 11 has freed himself of marking,
making use of 8's block and n° 6's movement to create space.
Teammates n° 5 and 9 attack the far post and the center in case
the cross goes longer.
After making the block, player n° 8 must be ready to intercept any
clearances in the center of the area.
N° 7 goes to occupy space outside the area to gather any
clearances and give preventive coverage.

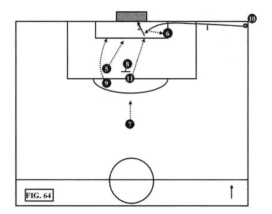

FIG. 64

Corner kick N° 7 (Fig. 65)

Player n° 10 takes the corner with an out-swinging trajectory towards 5, who has attacked space on the near post in anticipation.

When n° 5 gets to the ball, he flicks onto the far post towards 6, who had freed himself of marking making use of 11's block.

Teammates n° 8 and 9 attack the space behind n° 5 in case the cross goes long.

Having made the block, n° 11 must be ready to gather any clearances in the center of the area.

N° 7 goes to occupy space outside the area to get possession of any clearances and give preventive coverage.

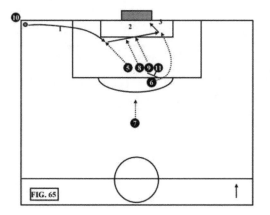

FIG. 65

Corner kick N° 8 (Fig. 66)

Player n° 10 takes a corner, kicking tight towards the edge of the area in the direction of n° 6, who has broken in from behind making use of n° 9, 8 and 11's movements to create space. You must take care to give n° 6 coverage in case he is anticipated or his shot is cleared (in this example such a task is carried out by n° 7).

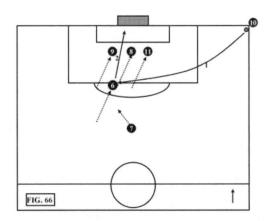

Corner kick N° 9 (Fig. 67)

The corner is taken by n° 10, who kicks tight with an out-swinging trajectory to the near post towards teammate n° 6 making use of 9, 8 and 11's movement to create space and 5's block.
Players n° 9, 8 and 11 attack the space in the center and on the far post in case the trajectory of the cross goes over n° 6's head.
Having made the block, n° 5 must be ready to pounce on any clearances in the center of the area.
N° 7 goes to occupy space outside the area to gather any clearances and give preventive coverage.

Corner kick n° 10 (fig. 68)

The corner is taken by player n° 10, who kicks tight and with an in-swinging trajectory into the central space in front of the goal towards n° 6.

N° 6 makes use of n° 5's block and the movements of 8, 11 and 9 (the first two attack the space on the near post, the third on the far post).

Having made the block, n° 5 must be ready to pounce on any clearances in the center of the area.

N° 7 goes to occupy space outside the area to gather any clearances and give preventive coverage.

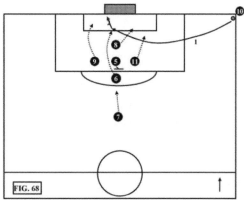

Corner kick N° 11 (fig. 69)

The corner is taken by player n° 10 with an in-swinging trajectory to the far post towards n° 5, who, after 11's veiling run, flicks with his head for his teammate n° 9's shot.

N° 8 attacks the space on the near post in case the pass is 'long', while n° 11 gives support for a possible back dump.

N° 7 goes to occupy space outside the area to gather any clearances and give preventive coverage.

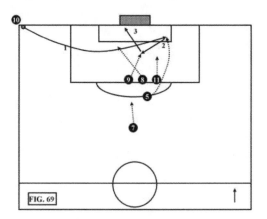

Corner kick N° 12 (Fig. 70)

The corner is taken
by n° 10 with a tight
out-swinging
trajectory to the near
post towards n° 9,
who has made use of
11's block.
Players n° 5 and 8
attack the center and
the far post in case
10's cross goes past
n° 9. N° 7 goes to
occupy space outside

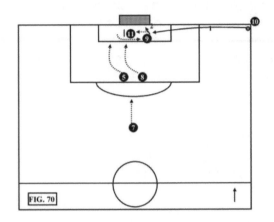

the area to gather any clearances and give preventive coverage.

Corner kick N° 13 (Fig. 71)

Player n° 10 takes the corner, passing back to n° 5 as he runs up.
N° 5 immediately crosses to the center with an out-swinging
trajectory towards n° 9.
N° 9 shoots after having moved to meet the ball, making use of 8's
veil into the space created by his own and 6 and 11's move to
break free of marking in the direction of the goal.
N° 7 goes to occupy space outside the area to gather any
clearances and give preventive coverage.

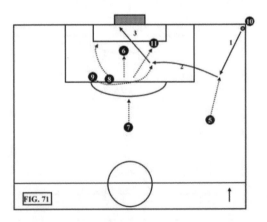

Corner kick N° 14 (Fig. 72)

The corner is taken by n° 10, kicking along the ground to n° 11, who, initially positioned on the near post, has gone to meet the ball.
When he has reached the ball, n° 11 passes back for n° 9, who shoots, having made use of 8's block.
N° 5 attacks the space on the far post in case the keeper clears or 9's shot is off the goal.
N° 7 goes to occupy space outside the area to gather any clearances and give preventive coverage.

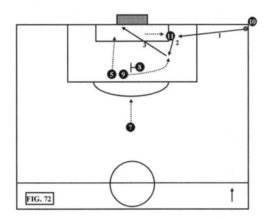

Corner kick N° 15 (Fig. 73)

The corner is taken by player n° 10, kicking to the near post with an out-swinging trajectory for n° 9, who shoots after making use of 8's block.

N° 5 attacks the space on the far post in case the keeper clears or 9's shot is off the goal.
N° 7 goes to occupy space outside the area to gather any clearances and give preventive coverage.

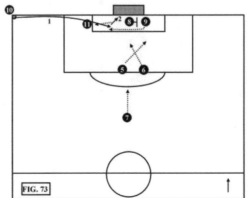

69

Corner kick N° 16 (fig. 74)

Player n° 10 takes the corner, passing straight along the ground towards n° 9, who has gone to meet the ball. N° 9 gives the ball back to 10, who makes a first touch in-swinging cross to the far post for n° 5. N. 5 has freed himself of marking making use of 11's block.

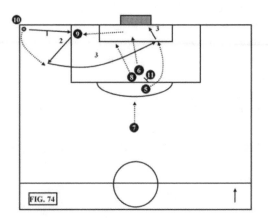

FIG. 74

Teammates n° 6 and 8 cut to attack the near post and the center in case 10's cross falls short.

Having carried out the block, n° 11 must be ready to pounce on any clearances the opponents might make in the area.

N° 7 goes to occupy space outside the area to gather any clearances and give preventive coverage.

Corner kick N° 17 (fig. 75)

Player n° 10 takes the corner, kicking to the center towards 8, who has made use of 9's veil.

N° 11 attacks the near post after 5's veil.

N° 7 goes to occupy space outside the area to gather any clearances and give preventive coverage.

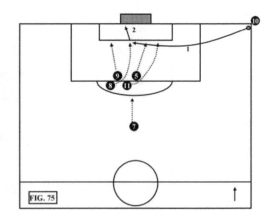

FIG. 75

Corner kick N° 18 (Fig. 76)

After having feinted a back pass towards n° 5, who is running up, player n° 10 takes the corner kick straight along the ground towards n° 9, who has gone to meet the ball.

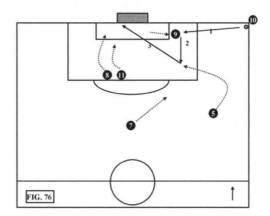

N° 9 passes to 5, who has in the meantime cut inside the area to receive the pass and shoot.
Teammates n° 8 and 11 attack the far post, both to free space for 5's shot and to shoot again should the first be off mark or if the keeper clears.
N° 7 goes to occupy space outside the area to gather any clearances and give preventive coverage.

Corner kick N° 19 (Fig. 77)

The corner is taken by n° 10.
Initially placed on a level with the penalty mark, teammates 8 and 11 attack respectively the near and the far post (11 veils for 8) freeing space in the center.
This space is then occupied by 9, 5 and 6.
At this point, N° 10 has five passing solutions.
In this example 10's in-swinging pass is for 5's shot on goal.
Players n° 8 and 11 must be ready to correct their teammates' mistaken trajectories and send any rebounds back into the net.
N° 7 goes to occupy space outside the area to gather any clearances and give preventive coverage.

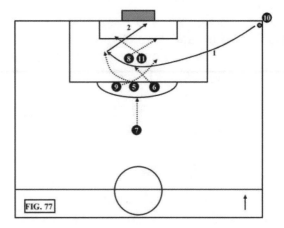

Corner kick N° 20 (Fig. 78)

Player n° 10 takes the corner, passing straight to n° 11, who has gone to meet the ball.
N° 11 feints a return pass to 10, but makes a sudden about turn and crosses for n° 8, who has attacked the near post.
N° 5 and 9 give 11 other passing solutions, respectively at the center and on the far post.
N° 7 goes to occupy space outside the area to gather any clearances and give preventive coverage.

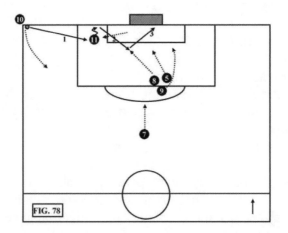

Corner kick N° 21 (Fig. 79)

Player n° 10 takes a corner, passing straight along the ground for n° 11, who has gone to meet the ball.

He returns the pass to 10, who feints a cross to the center, serving instead n° 8 as he runs up to the edge of the area, and 8 shoots.

Players 9, 6 and 5 get free of marking in the area to receive the cross, freeing space at the limit and creating a central corridor for 8's shot.

These three players must be ready to pounce on any rebounds following the shot.

N° 10 must decide carefully if it is possible to make an effective cross to n° 8: in cases where there are not the necessary conditions (i.e., the edges of the area are occupied by opponents or n° 8 is tightly marked) he must go for a cross to the center for 9, 6 or 5.

N° 7 goes to occupy space outside the area to gather any clearances and give preventive coverage.

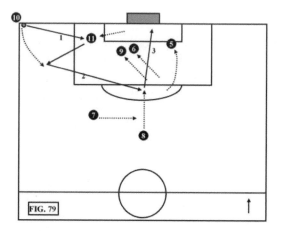

FIG. 79

Corner kick N° 22 (Fig. 80)

The corner is taken by n° 10, feinting a straight pass along the ground for n° 11, but then crossing to the center with an in-swinging trajectory towards 6, who has broken in using his teammates 9, 8 and 5's movements to create space.

These players must be ready both to head the ball in case the cross is not precise for n° 6 and to catch any possible clearances by the opponents after the shot.

N° 7 goes to occupy space outside the area to gather any clearances and give preventive coverage.

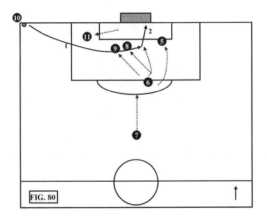

Corner kick N° 23 (fig. 81)

N° 10 takes the corner with an out-swinging trajectory to the near post towards n° 6, who has broken free of marking using 8's block. Players n° 9 and 5 attack the zone around the far post in case the cross goes over n° 6's head, and they must be ready to correct 6's shot if it is off target.

Initially, player n° 11 makes it difficult for the opposing keeper to come out, and then he goes to the far post.

Having carried out the block, n° 8 has the job of trying to take possession of the opponents' clearances in the area. N° 7 goes to occupy space outside the area to gather any clearances and give preventive coverage.

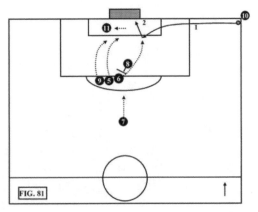

Corner kick N° 24 (Fig. 82)

The corner is taken by player n° 10.
The four teammates who are to receive the cross position themselves close together and in a horizontal line.
This type of placement is the best set up for veils and blocks. In this particular play, n° 9 and n° 5 make use of the veils of 8 and 6.
Four spaces are occupied in the area: the near and the far post, the right and the left center.
The player taking the kick has four pass solutions: in this example the out-swinging cross is for n° 9's shot. He has attacked the left center.
The initial horizontal placement of the receiving players allows you to structure many different solutions.
N° 7 goes to occupy space outside the area to gather any clearances and give preventive coverage.

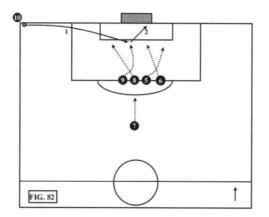

Corner kick N° 25 (Fig. 83)

The corner is taken by n° 10. The four teammates who will be receiving the cross place themselves close together in a vertical line.
This initial layout allows for veils and blocks to be carried out in the best possible way. In this particular play the four receivers veil for each other (a player veils for the one behind him and uses the veil of the player in front).
Four spaces are occupied in the area: the near and the far post, the right and the left center.

The player taking the kick has four passing solutions: in this example the in-swinging cross is for n° 9's shot - he has attacked the far post. The initial horizontal placement of the receiving players allows you to structure many different solutions.

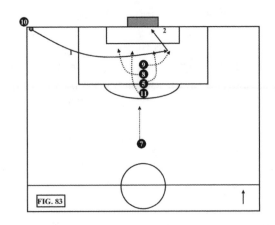

N° 7 goes to occupy space outside the area to gather any clearances and give preventive coverage.

Corner kick N° 26 (Fig. 84)

Player n° 10 takes the corner with a tight out-swinging trajectory to the near post for n° 11, who makes use of 8's block and 5's movement to create space.

Teammates n° 6 and 9 free themselves of marking in the center of the area in case n° 10's cross is too far back, and they must also be ready to pounce on any rebound.

Having carried out the block, player n° 8 has to try and correct any mistaken trajectories on the far post and the keeper's clearance.

N° 7 goes to occupy space outside the area to gather any clearances and give preventive coverage.

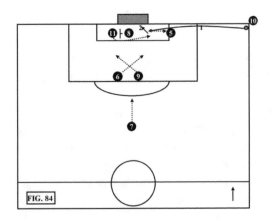

Corner kick N° 27 (Fig. 85)

The corner is taken by n° 10, who kicks tight and with an in-swinging trajectory to the far post for n° 9, who has made use of 8's block and 5's movement to create space on the far post. Player n° 6 attacks the space behind them and on the near post, and must be

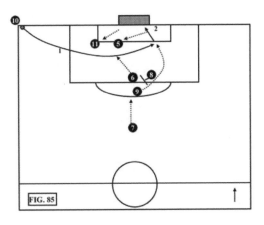

FIG. 85

ready both for short trajectories and for the opponents' clearances.
N° 5's job is to put the rebound into the back of the net.
N° 11 must flick the cross on if it is short and correct the shot if it is off goal.
N° 7 goes to occupy space outside the area to gather any clearances and give preventive coverage.

Corner kick N° 28 (Fig. 86)

The corner is taken by player n° 10, kicking tight and with an out-swinging trajectory towards n° 5, who has freed himself of marking centrally.
N° 5 has made use of the space created by the movements of 6 (attacking the far post) and 8 (attacking the near post), as well as 8's veil.
Initially player n° 9 goes to meet the ball, ready to flick it towards the center if the trajectory is short; he then turns towards the goal to deviate shots off center and to cover any rebound.
At the start, player n° 11 must make it difficult for the keeper to come out; he will then move onto the far post to receive trajectories towards this zone and to shoot back the opposing n° 1's clearances.
N° 7 goes to occupy space outside the area to gather any clearances and give preventive coverage.

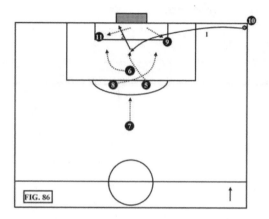

FIG. 86

Corner kick N° 29 (Fig. 87)

The corner is taken by player n° 10, kicking tight and with an in-swinging trajectory towards n° 6 who has freed himself of marking on the far post.

N° 6 has made use of the movements of 5 (attacking the space in the center) and 8 (attacking the near post), as well as 8's veil.

Initially, player n° 11 goes to meet the ball, ready to flick it towards the center if the trajectory is short; he then turns towards the goal to deviate off center shots into the goal and to cover any rebound.

Player n° 9 frees space on the far post, moving in the direction of the center of the goal, ready to shoot back the keeper's clearances.

N° 7 goes to occupy space outside the area to gather any clearances and give preventive coverage.

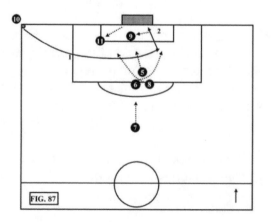

FIG. 87

Corner kick N° 30 (Fig. 88)

The corner is taken by player n° 10, kicking tight with an in-swinging trajectory towards n° 9, who has freed himself of marking on the far post making use of 8's block.

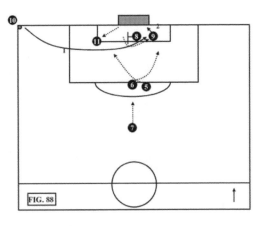

FIG. 88

Initially, player n° 11 goes to meet the ball, ready to flick it towards the center if the trajectory is short; he then turns towards the goal to deviate off center shots into the goal and to cover any rebound.

Teammates n° 6 and 5 free themselves of marking in the center of the area in case n° 10's cross is too far back; they must also be ready to gather the opponents' clearances.

Having carried out the block, it is 8's job to jump on any rebounds. N° 7 goes to occupy space outside the area to gather any clearances and give preventive coverage.

Corner kick N° 31 (Fig. 89)

The receiving players position themselves in the center to form a double triangle.

Player n° 10 takes the corner, kicking tight with an out-swinging trajectory on the near post towards 9, who has freed himself of marking using 8's block.

In cases where the cross goes over n° 9's head, the other three players have attacked the other spaces in the area in this way: n° 11 on the right center, n° 6 on the left center and n° 5 on the far post.

Having carried out his block, n° 8 must be ready to grab hold of the opponents' clearances in the area.

N° 7 goes to occupy space outside the area to gather any clearances and give preventive coverage.

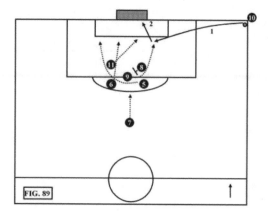

FIG. 89

Corner kick N° 32 (Fig. 90)

The corner is taken by n° 10.
N° 11 and 5, positioned respectively on the first and the far post, make a movement backwards to free space for engagement.
Players n° 9, 8 and 6 attack space, getting free of marking respectively at the center and on the near and far post.
The player taking the kick will then have 3 passing solutions: in this example the in-swinging trajectory of 10's cross favors n° 9's shot, 9 having freed himself of marking in the center.
Having created space, teammates n° 11 and 5 must be ready to intercept the opponents' clearances in the area.
N° 7 goes to occupy space outside the area to gather any clearances and give preventive coverage.

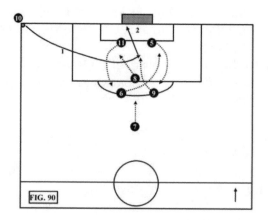

FIG. 90

Corner kick N° 33 (Fig. 91)

Player n° 10 takes the corner along the ground towards n° 9, who has gone to meet the ball after making use of 5's veil.

When n° 9 has reached the ball, he immediately crosses tight on the far post with an out-swinging trajectory for n° 8, who has used 11's block.

Having veiled for 9, n° 5 then frees himself of marking in the center in case the cross is short.

Having made the block, player n° 11 must be ready to grab hold of the opponents' clearances in the area.

N° 7 goes to occupy space outside the area to gather any clearances and give preventive coverage.

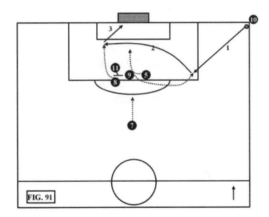

FIG. 91

Corner kick N° 34 (Fig. 92)

The corner is taken by n° 10.

The five receivers position themselves in this way: two at the level of the penalty mark and the other three at the edge of the area.

The receivers go to attack five different spaces: 9 and 8 go for, respectively, the far and the near post (9 veils for 8); 6, 5 and 11 for the central spaces slightly behind.

The player taking the corner therefore has 5 passing solutions: in this example, 6 has used 11's veil and 10's in-swinging cross is for him.

N° 7 goes to occupy space outside the area to gather any clearances and give preventive coverage.

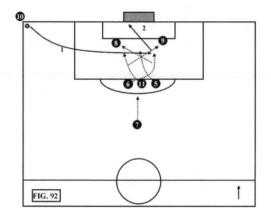

Corner kick n° 35 (Fig. 93)

Player n° 10 takes the corner.
The 4 receivers group themselves at the edge of the area.
This placement makes it difficult for the opponents to mark, and also favors the natural development of blocks and veils.
The receivers must then 'open up', going to attack the following spaces in the area: the near and far post, the right and left center.
In this example, n° 10's out-swinging cross is for n° 8's shot.
N° 7 goes to occupy space outside the area to gather any clearances and give preventive coverage.

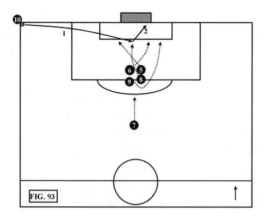

The throw in

The throw in is a stationary ball situation that takes place frequently during a match.
It is imperative, therefore, to organize the way play starts up on these occasions so that you get more effective attacking play.
You must structure organized movements that will put a player in position to carry out good finishing touches. It goes without saying that the throw in will also have to be coached from a technical point of view, above all in the youth sector, where it is a good idea to use exercises aim at improving the basic techniques.
In the attacking zone it is very important to have a player good at making long throws, forming movements to break free of marking and creating space in the area. In the defense zone, on the other hand, it is better to go for less risky solutions, tending to keep possession (the most widely used play is the return pass to the player who has thrown in). In the following pages we will be illustrating attacking schemes when balls go out of play principally in the offensive zone or the mid field.

Plays

Throw in N° 1 (Fig. 94)

N° 6 throws in from the attacking half, serving n° 9 who has come to meet the ball.
N° 9 lays off to supporting player n° 8, who passes along the flank to n° 6 as he breaks on the side.
N° 6 then crosses on the near post for 11, who shoots.

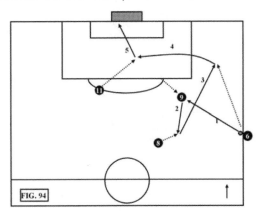

FIG. 94

Throw in N° 2 (Fig. 95)

N° 5 throws in towards 10, who has gone to meet the ball.
He lays off to 11, who has broken in along the flank.
Player n° 11 crosses on the far post towards 9, who shoots.

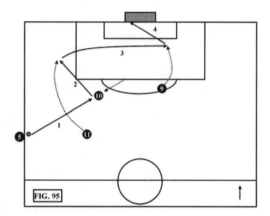

Throw in N° 3 (Fig. 96)

N° 6 throws in, serving n° 5, who has cut in after a crossover with
11
N° 5 then crosses tight on the far post towards 10, who shoots after
making use of n° 9's block.

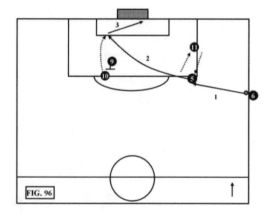

Throw in N° 4 (Fig. 97)

Player n° 5 throws in towards n° 10.
N° 10 dummies in favor of n° 9, who then passes to 10 as he breaks in along the flank.
Player n° 10 then crosses on the far post for 11's shot.

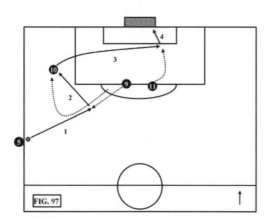

Throw in n° 5 (Fig. 98)

Player n° 6 throws in towards 11, who has come to meet the ball.
He then dumps back to supporting player n° 10, who re-launches along the flank where 5 has broken in.
N° 5 crosses to the center on the near post for n° 8's shot.

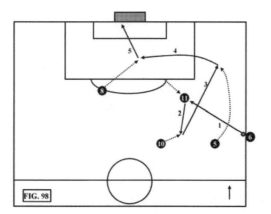

Throw in N° 6 (Fig. 99)

The throw in is taken by n° 6. N° 10 moves to meet the ball and then breaks in along the flank. The throw in reaches n° 11, who passes to 10. 10 then crosses on the far post for n° 9, who shoots.

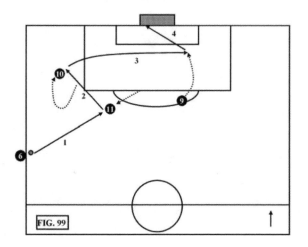

Throw in N° 7 (fig. 100)

Player n° 6 throws in to n° 9, who has come to meet the ball. He passes to his teammate n° 11, who has cut into the field.
N° 11 passes to 10, and he shoots.

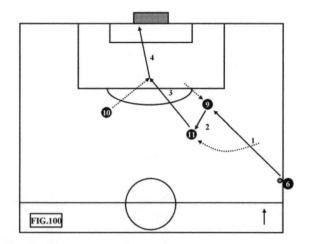

Throw in N° 8 (Fig. 101)

Player n° 6 throws in towards 11, who has come to meet the ball. He passes back to supporting player n° 10, who feints a pass along the flank to n° 5, and then changes play for n° 8 as he breaks in. N° 8 then crosses to the center on the far post for his teammate n° 9's shot.

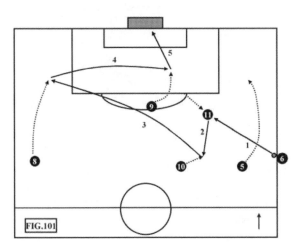

Throw in N° 9 (Fig. 102)

Player n° 6 throws in towards n° 8, who returns the ball to him. N° 6 then re-launches n° 10 who has broken in on the flank.
N° 10 crosses on the near post for teammate n° 11, who shoots.

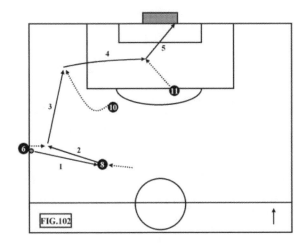

Throw in n° 10 (Fig. 103)

N° 5 throws in towards 10, who has come to meet the ball. N° 10 feints a pass to n° 11, and stops the in-swinging ball instead, then crosses onto the far post in 7's direction as he breaks into the space left free by 9.

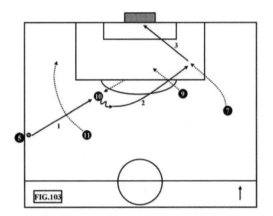

Throw in N° 11 (Fig. 104)

Player n° 6 throws in.
The two receivers, n° 9 and n° 11, crossover - giving n° 6 two passing solutions.
In this example, the ball reaches n° 9, who crosses to the center on the near post where n° 10 has freed himself of marking.
N° 5 attacks the far post, giving the player making the cross another option.

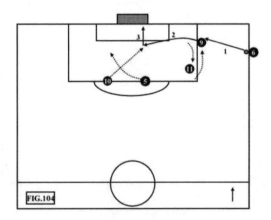

Throw in N° 12 (Fig. 105)

N° 6 throws in towards 11, who has come to meet the ball.
He then passes to n° 10, who crosses onto the far post towards n° 9.
N° 9 flicks with his head for n° 8, who shoots.

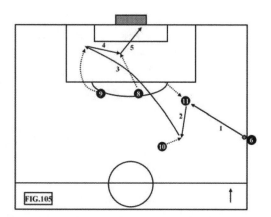

Throw in N° 13 (Fig. 106)

N° 10 throws in serving n° 9 in depth, who has gone to meet the ball.
N° 9 flicks to his teammates n° 8, 11 and 5, who are attacking space in the area.
In this example, n° 9's flick is foe n° 5's shot.

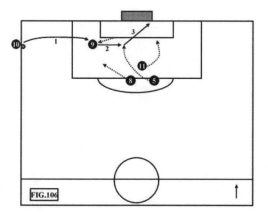

Throw in N° 14 (Fig. 107)

Player n° 6 throws in serving n° 11 on the flank, who has broken in using 5's movement to create space as he comes to meet the ball. N° 11 then crosses to the center on the near post for his teammate n° 10.
N° 9 attacks the far post, giving 11 another solution for his cross.

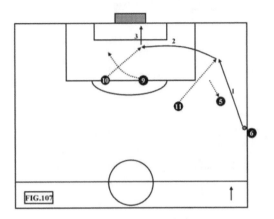

FIG.107

Throw in N° 15 (Fig. 108)

N° 6 throws in serving n° 10, who has come to meet the ball. He rebounds on 5, who shoots. The two teammates n° 11 and n° 9 attack space on the far post to correct the trajectories of the shots in case they are off target.

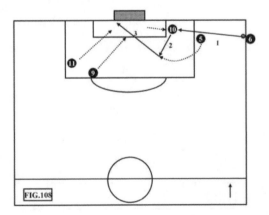

FIG.108

90

Throw in N° 16 (Fig. 109)

Player n° 10 throws in towards n° 11, who has crossed over with n° 5. N° 11has two passing solutions: back along the ground to n° 5, who has got free of marking towards the center of the area, or on the far post to n° 9. In this example, n° 11 serves his teammate n° 5, who shoots.

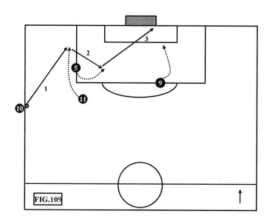

Throw in N° 17 (Fig. 110)

N° 6 throws in serving n° 9 in the area, who has freed himself of marking in the empty space created by n° 11 and n° 5's crossover and making use of 8's block. N° 9 can immediately shoot or serve n° 10, who has attacked the zone on the far post. In cases where 9 shoots directly, n° 10 must be ready to deflect if the trajectory is off target.

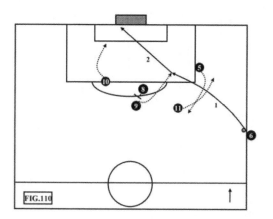

Throw in N° 18 (Fig. 111)

N° 8 takes the throw in, sending the ball high to n° 10, who has come to meet it.
N° 10 flicks the ball for 9 as he breaks in having crossed over with n° 11.
Player n° 9 now has three playing solutions:
- ♦ A direct shot on goal;
- ♦ A side pass along the ground for 11's shot;
- ♦ A pass onto the far post for n° 5's shot.

In this example n° 9 goes for the last solution.

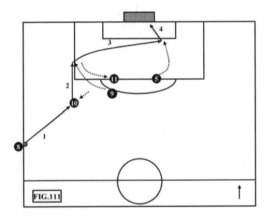

Throw in N° 19 (Fig. 112)

N° 6 throws in, serving n° 8, who has crossed over with 5.
N° 8 then crosses to the edge of the area towards n° 9, who shoots having attacked the free space created by 10 and 11's movements. They have to be ready to pounce on any rebounds.

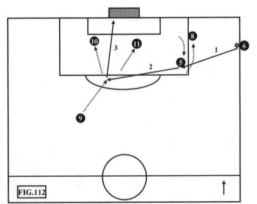

Throw in N° 20 (Fig. 113)

Player n° 3 throws in.
N° 10 makes a movement to meet the ball, changing direction and receiving 3's throw in by using 11's feint.
N° 10 can shoot directly or pass to his teammate n° 5 on the far post.
In cases where 10 shoots directly, n° 5 must be ready to correct any trajectories that are off target.

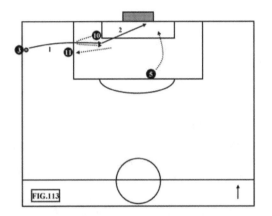

FIG.113

Penalty kicks

The shot from eleven meters is very effective as far as goal scoring is concerned. The percentage of goals netted is much higher in these situations than on any other stationary balls.
The penalty kick can be taken in different ways.
  ♦ Using force
  ♦ Using precision
  ♦ Using cunning
It follows that the ability to trick the keeper is as important as the precision and the speed of the shot.
The best run up to take before the shot is the diagonal, which makes it easier for the player kicking the penalty to hide his real intentions than a straight run up.
Fig. 14 shows the correct run up for n° 10, the player taking a penalty, with the teammates at the edge of the area ready to grab hold of a possible clearance by the keeper or a rebound off the posts.

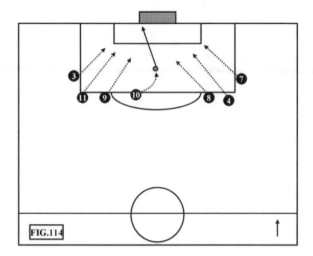

FIG.114

Apart from the technical aspect, the psychological element is of the utmost importance in this type of dead ball situation.

The ability to keep your cool on the penalty mark is fundamental for the successful outcome of the kick - you must not be subject to any outside conditioning but must concentrate on the execution of the shot itself.

It often happens, in fact, that players with inferior technical skills manage to score on penalties because they have good personality and are confident.

These players are better able to control their emotions in stressful situations, showing greater calm and composure.

TEACHING AND EXERCISES

Teaching methods for coaching dead ball situations in attack are part of more general methods used for the offensive phase.

The offensive phase can be coached in two main ways:

1) Coaching by using schemes;
2) Coaching by using situations.

Coaching the attacking phase using schemes means doing exercises in which the opponents are not present. Situational training, on the other hand, foresees the presence of active opposition.

When using coaching by schemes, therefore, we are working in a simplified reality, in our own spaces and at our own times, which is not true of situational training.

Because the opponents are missing, the first method aims to produce automatic reactions and feeling between players, and to develop a strong attacking mentality.

When the team has digested the movements to be made on the field, you can go on to coach the attacking phase in situations, at the same time putting on more and more opponents.

We therefore advise you to start off by coaching the various dead ball situations without the presence of opponents, in 11 against 0 situations where you will be organizing both the actual movements of the receivers and the timing of those movements in connection with the moment the player takes the kick or throws in from the sidelines.

It is very important as well to indicate the useful positions for those players who are not directly involved in the set play, but who are playing a vital role as preventive cover.

You can see in Fig. 115 the placement of the team for a corner kick.

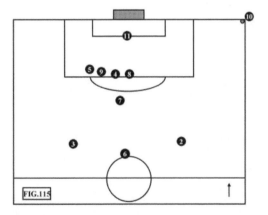

After this first stage, you will be carrying out exercises with the presence of opponents, who will be semi-active to start off, then active - this will make it more difficult to carry out the play, which will now become more and more similar to actual match situations.

In my opinion it is not a good idea to concentrate all coaching on dead balls in one period of the training session (this is almost always the section connected with finishing touches).

Remember that the players' concentration declines visibly after 15 minutes and you will see that it is better to coach them during the whole week, inserting various dead ball situations between one exercise and another, even during the same session.

As I see it, the following is the most suitable situational exercise for the type of methods I have been explaining: you play an 11 against 11 match on a full-sized field, (or an 8 against 8 on one half of a field), in which play is always started from a dead ball situation.

The two teams must take turns in attack and defend, changing every 2 minutes. Their aim, of course, is to shoot on goal at the end of an action, but you must also be looking for tactical balance in the negative or positive transition phase.

Fig. 116 illustrates an 8 against 8 match in one half of a field where play is starting off from an indirect free kick.

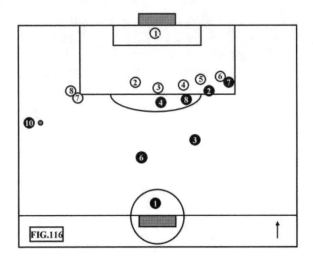

FIG.116

CHAPTER 4

DEAD BALL SITUATIONS IN DEFENSE

We will now have a look at dead ball situations during the defense phase, beginning, as we did with the attacking phase, by considering the general principles and the individual technical and tactical skills in the players who are defending, and then going on to analyze the defensive strategies available in every restart situation.

GENERAL PRINCIPLES

Concentration of the defense

By defensive concentration, we mean the way playing space is closed up and restricted so as to make the opponents' maneuvers more difficult to carry out.

The defending team must close itself as a 'funnel', which means that as the opponents get nearer to the goal, the defending players have to close the spaces in front of it to cover the central zone, which is always the most dangerous. This principle is valid even as far as dead balls are concerned. There is an illustration in Fig. 117 of the tight, short defensive layout of a team that is trying to contrast an opposing in-depth free kick.

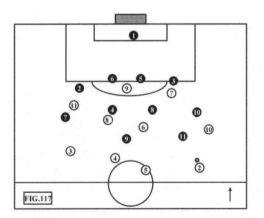

Numerical superiority

The most important aim of a team in the defense phase is to create numerical superiority near the ball, in relation to the goal and to the position of the teammates and the opponents.

To create that, the team must shorten in towards the ball, tightly mark the opponents near it and control in anticipation those who are further away, working on the interception of the passes.

Naturally, this principle is just as important when you are talking about restarts.

These are particularly dangerous situations, and the players must pay special attention to defending the goal, above all as concerns corners, free kicks and throw ins in the attacking zone. In other words, the coach must give his team instruction on how to create numerical superiority in the zone of the field where the opponents' ball will probably be directed, always keeping in mind the principle that the goal is to be defended at all costs.

In Fig. 118 you can see a throw in situation in the attacking zone, in which the defending team positions itself correctly to create numerical superiority both near the ball and in the center of the area in order to defend the goal.

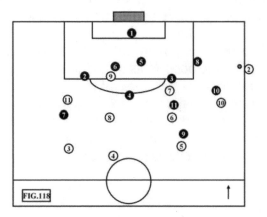

FIG.118

Space and time

Space and time are the two most important variables in the game of soccer.

Soccer is a situational sport, and a good coach must be able during training to give his players the right methods allowing them to read and interpret the various scenarios that can emerge on the field so as to obtain suitable responses in relation to the concepts of space and time, and to the defensive strategy he has adopted for the team.

Covering the spaces is a very important defensive action which will allow the team to regain possession by intercepting poor passes by the opponents and set possession of loose balls.

Organized defensive movements carried out by the team with the right timing in order to occupy and close off spaces in a rational way are things that the coach will need to work on with care and determination.

It goes without saying that these concepts are highly applicable to dead ball situations as well.

In such cases, all the players must have been given training in how to read the situation consistently in order to occupy the positions on the field in the most effective way and to limit the playing spaces.

Marking the opponents correctly, concentrating men in defense, creating numerical superiority, pressing and offside tactics are all elements that aim to reduce time and space in the opponents' maneuvers.

Positive transition

Positive transition is the change from the defensive to the attacking phase, after having regained possession.

As we have already said, statistics show that an increasing number of goals are scored following a so-called break, i.e., after a quick counter attack subsequent to the opponents losing possession.

It follows that the coach must train this important third phase as well as he can, inserting exercises in his schedules that aim to develop and improve his players' individual and collective skills in passing rapidly and effectively from the non possession to the possession phase.

Your objective is to organize active and resourceful defensive strategies, structuring the collaborative mechanisms leading to the fast and effective recovery of possession first of all, and then, when that has taken place, to rapid and well thought-out counter-attacking plays. You can see in Fig. 119 an organized counter-attack starting out from the keeper who has gained possession of the ball after a free kick by the opponents.

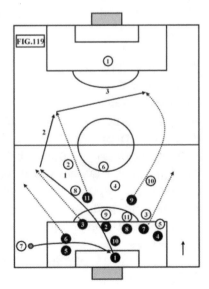

FIG.119

Marking the zone

In zonal play, each player is responsible for the zone of the field that has been assigned to him and for the opponents who find themselves in that particular part of the area of play.

A player not in possession must also control the nearby zones and put pressure on any opponent with the ball who enters his zone.

In order to get the best organization of the defense phase following the principles of zonal play, the coach must first of all underline the main points of reference in order of importance: i.e., the ball, the teammates and the opponents.

The most important point of reference is the position of the ball, in second place the teammates, and lastly the opponents.

An organized team will therefore move in a coordinated (with the right timing), compact (keeping tight and short) way on the basis of the ball's movements, and in relation to the position of teammates and opponents, respecting the distances between both the sections themselves and the individual players in each section.

As we have already seen, the most important priority to follow is the creation of numerical superiority around the ball, which can be obtained by shortening the team near it, tightly marking the opponents closest to it when it is covered (i.e., pressed) and controlling those further away in anticipation, working on the interception of the trajectories of the passes.

The coach must talk to his men, training and encouraging them to 'think and act collectively' so that they can make uniform readings of the various situations of play.

You can establish defensive strategies based on zonal marking also on dead balls.

In these cases all the players have to occupy a pre-defined zone, so as to create the right concentration of men in the space to be defended, in which each player has the job of attacking the ball and looking after the particular space assigned to him.

In using this marking system, you naturally tend to favor the occupation of space and the right marking on the opponents who will take up position in those spaces, so reducing the danger coming from their movements as they try to create room for themselves.

This is a choice that makes your own players more independent of the opponents.

The players will have to worry about spaces, trajectories, position, coverage, the goal, the ball, their organization and, last of all, the opponents (as a consequence of all the other factors).

That does not mean that you can underestimate the opponents' behavior, but only that it is not the main focus.

Using this type of marking, you must try to involve all your players in defense.

When talking about occupying space and intercepting trajectories, you need to be able to use the greatest number of players possible.

Fig. 120 shows how to position players in defense when the opponents are taking a free kick in the attacking zone.

N° 2 and 7 place themselves in the wall, while the players at the center move back first of all and then go to attack the ball. N° 4 follows the backward movement of the line, and it is his job to 'hunt out' any possible clearances, while n° 9 stays in depth, not participating directly in the defense, but ready in case there is a break or a long clearance.

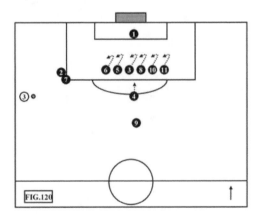

FIG.120

Mixed marking

This type of defense solution foresees some players going in individual marking on some opponents, while others are principally occupying special spaces.

In situations with the ball in movement, this defensive strategy usually calls for the presence of two defenders that mark the opposing strikers man to man. They are protected by a sweeper in coverage, and the other teammates mark the zone.

On stationary ball situations, mixed marking has some players in individual marking on predefined opponents, while others are covering those predetermined spaces that are considered particularly dangerous, as well as giving coverage to those marking the man.

This type of defense marking is a strategic choice half way between zonal and man to man marking because it uses personal marking of some opponents - usually those who are particularly good at aerial play - while at the same time occupying spaces, which, if left free, could lead to dangerous situations for the team (e.g., the zone around the first and the far post). In Fig. 121 you can see the placement of a team that is using mixed marking on a corner taken by the opponents.

N° 11 places himself at the regular distance from the ball to disturb the cross, while n° 10 takes up position on the near post.

Players n° 6 and 3 occupy the space in front of the first and far post on a level with the goal area, ready to attack the ball by following its trajectory.

N° 2, 4 and 5 are marking their men in the center of the area, whose job it will be to receive the cross, while n° 7 and 9 take up position at the edge of the area, ready to grab hold of clearances.

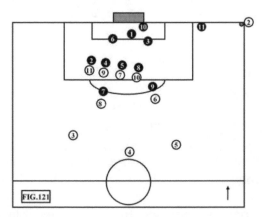

FIG.121

Man to man marking

This is a defense solution in which each player in defense uses personal marking on a predetermined opponent. In situations when the ball is in movement, there is also a sweeper, whose job it is to cover for his teammates in cases where they have been beaten.

On dead balls the sweeper can position himself on the post, mark up (if he is good at aerial play), or stay in the center of the area 'hunting' for the cross. The choice of rigorously marking the man on free kicks is not a very common one because you will be following the opponents without worrying at all about occupying space. In that way, you come to depend too much on your opponents, and do not have an active, resourceful defensive attitude. You can see in Fig. 122 a situation on an opponents' side free kick. All the players except the two in the wall are marking their own direct opponents man to man.

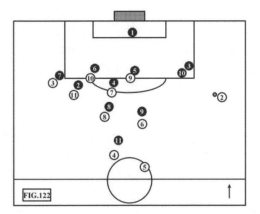

FIG.122

Pressing

Pressing is a collective defense action that aims to limit the opponent's playing space and time in their maneuvers. In contrast, pressure is an individual defense action by which a player limits an opponent's space and time as he receives the ball in the defender's zone. It follows, therefore, that, while you can have pressure without pressing, you cannot have pressing without pressure on the opposing player in possession. The compactness of the team is an indispensable condition when you wish to apply effective, organized pressing, which means that the players must be placed correctly on the field, respecting the distance between the sections and between the members of each single section. Being aggressive with the opponents in possession is an important feature of a team, which will force them to play in difficult conditions and on horizontal lines because their vertical maneuvers will be blocked off. Pressing is therefore an important instrument for taking back possession, but it must be carried out rationally and with good organization because it is physically very tiring, and, keeping in mind the positions that the players must take up on the field (tight and anticipatory marking on the ball possessor's supporting players), it does not allow for the creation of suitable lines of cover in relation to the ball. For these reasons, a team that is using pressing must be in excellent physical condition, and must be good at moving in and shortening up on the ball with the right timing, knowing that any delay or mistake in position during these defense moves will allow an opponent to come out and receive a dump, which, in turn, will create a favorable playing situation for the attack. Pressing is an important way of regaining possession on dead balls as well, above all with throw ins, clearances following corners, free kicks and when the opposing keeper puts the ball back into play.

Offside

An important way of regaining ball possession, offside tactics can be active or passive. In the first case, the opponents' offside position is brought about by the whole defense section moving into depth. In the second, you get offside because an opposing striker moves beyond the defense line, which is not moving into depth (and here the important thing is the zonal defender's 'follow and ditch' movement in connection with the opponent who goes beyond the line).

Active offside tactics are collective defense plays which must be used with astuteness and organization, above all as concerns lower amateur categories and the youth sector, where the fact that there are no linesmen to assist the referees makes it difficult to evaluate whether a player is really in an offside position or not.

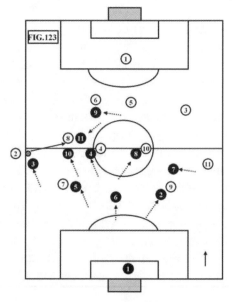

The fact is that if you make a mistake in carrying out offside tactics, you may be putting the opponents in a position of advantage, because one of their players will come face to face with the keeper. To make this defense action as effective as possible, what you need is to put pressure on the ball.

If the defense moves into depth to apply offside on an uncovered ball, that might create problems for our team because the opposing player in possession will then be able to choose the playing solution that suits him best without being attacked and with the defenders finding themselves in depth and without reciprocal coverage.

The defense line must be in a position to decide jointly about covered and uncovered balls, moving up or back appropriately, while at the same time handling any later attempts by the opposing mid fielders to break into space.

The keeper plays an important role in carrying out offside because when the defense is moving up he must place himself correctly and in a forward position so as to carry out his work as an extra sweeper.

The most important thing is for the coach to establish the strategy to be used on these tactics, carefully defining the situations and the zones of the field in which it is to be carried out.

Offside is a defense solution that is also used in dead ball situations, almost exclusively during the opponents' free kicks.

For example, if we are facing opponents who are better than us at aerial play, on free kicks the coach can organize a forward movement by the team in order to put the opponents in an offside position.

The defenders' movement out must come about with the right timing, i.e., when the player taking the kick is beginning his run up and has lowered his eyes on the ball. This defense situation is illustrated in Fig. 124.

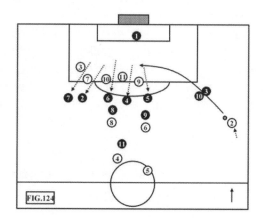

FIG.124

INDIVIDUAL TECHNICAL AND TACTICAL SKILLS

Taking up position or placement

This consists in positioning yourself in relation to your goal, your direct opponent and the section of the field where the ball is in transit, in such a way as to give you the chance to delay or obstruct the opponents' play.

As the opponents get nearer to the goal - i.e., the danger zone - each defender must place himself in such a way as to give priority to defending his own goal.

Each player in defense has to take up an internal position with respect to the goal, thus putting the opponent on the outside. This means that he will have to cover less distance than his opponent, being careful at all times not to be taken by surprise in the blind zone, i.e., from behind.

By placing himself correctly and having less distance to cover, he cancels not only the advantage that the opponent had in his initiative, but also the fact that his speed of movement may initially have been greater.

The defender's behavior must be active, aiming to get the striker to occupy a space that will be less dangerous should there be a shot, always keeping in mind the opponent's individual skills and the position in which he operates on the field.

The defender will have to put his body crosswise to the opponent in a position from which he can see the ball and the striker at the same time.

Putting defensive safety first, the back will have to foresee the chance of intercepting and gaining possession of a ball passed to his direct opponent.

It goes without saying that this kind of individual tactical skill will also be necessary for collective defensive play in dead ball situations, above all on those (corners, free kicks and throw ins from in-depth zones) in which the placement of the defenders is taking place in a danger zone, i.e., near their own goal.

Marking

Marking is strictly connected to placement.
Being able to mark an opponent means looking out carefully for his

movements, keeping at a suitable distance and in the right position to hinder or limit his attacking action by contrasting or anticipating his movements.

The correct distance to be kept from a direct opponent depends not only on the defender's and the striker's skills (e.g., it is possible to mark the striker tightly if the defender is faster), but also and above all on the position of the ball with respect to both the goal and the opponent.

As the ball gets nearer his own goal, the defender's marking must get tighter and tighter, while, when the striker is far away from the ball, the marking can be loosened up.

Correct marking is a necessary individual skill for effective defense in dead ball situations.

Above all on free kicks where the opponents are to be marked in a dangerous zone, the defender must anticipate the attacker and keep in close contact (at the distance of an outstretched arm) to him at the edge and inside the area, making sure that he cannot cut away and avoid interception. If he is outside the area it is better to wait for him from inside, placing yourself so as to be able to anticipate with respect to the ball.

Fig. 125 shows the correct placement of the defenders in marking in connection with the position of their direct opponent.

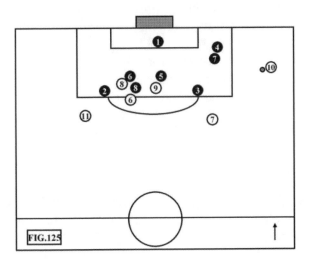

FIG.125

Intercepting

The natural consequence of suitable placement and correct marking is you will be able to intercept the ball.

Interception happens when the defender interrupts the opponents' attacking play by going in directly on the ball.

The most frequent and effective type of interception is without any doubt when a player anticipates a striker who is about to receive the ball, and takes possession of it.

In order for the interception to be successful, the defender will not only have to place himself and mark correctly, but must also time things perfectly and be able to accelerate.

Interception can be followed by a number of plays - a clearance in situations of danger, a direct pass to a teammate or a simple change of direction by the foot or by the head.

As we have just said, interception is a good way of regaining possession, but the defender must be very good at carrying it out because if he messes it up he will have freed the striker of marking.

Anticipation must very often be used in situations on inactive balls, above all in the dangerous zone and as a consequence of the type of (anticipatory) marking used.

Allowing your direct opponent to receive the ball inside or near the area can create a situation of risk for your team. The defender who anticipates the opponent in the area as the free kick develops will then have to go for safety, passing to a free teammate or clearing the ball out of the area.

In this last case, it is better if the defender clears the ball as far away as possible and to the sides, so reducing to a minimum the chance of the opponents shooting from outside the area.

You can see in Fig. 126 an interception followed by a clearance along the flank made by a defender in marking on a side free kick.

Contrasting

The defender will not always be able to regain possession by intercepting. He will often have to try and take the ball away from an opponent by tackling.

Tackling means taking the ball away from an opponent in possession.

The timing of the intervention is what makes this individual defensive play so effective. The defender must be able to choose the moment when the opponent has lost control, when he is not placing his body in defense of the ball or in cases where he tries to dribble past.

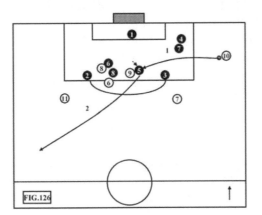

FIG.126

There are two types of contrast:
- Direct: when the defender intervenes directly on an opponent in possession;
- Indirect: when the defender positions himself in such a way as to put his direct opponent in the 'shadow zone', i.e., unable to receive a pass onto his feet

We have already said that the best defensive play on dead balls in the danger zone is the interception, but it is also true that good contrasting skills are necessary when the opponent has already received the ball.

In this last case, the defender will have to contrast by placing himself in defense of the goal, staying on his feet (i.e., not going for a sliding tackle) and concentrating on the ball, trying to intervene on the spur of the moment so as not to give the player in possession the time and freedom to shoot at goal from inside the area.

Playing for time

The defender does not always try to regain possession by intercepting, contrasting or tackling. Sometimes it is better to play for time to get an upper hand on the opponents' maneuver.

Playing for time is very useful when the defender finds himself having to face a situation of numerical inferiority.

By playing for time the defender gives his teammates the chance to get back into position so that they can recreate a situation of at least numerical equality.

In addition, it is a good idea to play for time when you are facing a striker who is very good at dribbling.

In dead ball situations, you play for time above all when the ball will not be played into the danger zone.

Exchange of marking

This is a combined defensive play made by at least two players, and its aim is to re-establish the defensive balance that might have been lost on account of the opponents' movements.

This type of defensive play is very useful on dead ball situations to not give even the minimum space to the opponents, above all near the goal.

Exchange of marking is very handy in situations where an opponent is blocking in favor of a teammate.

As you can see in Fig. 127, the player marking the opponent that is making the block must go and mark the player who is using that block, while the other defender looks after the one who is obstructing.

Exchange of marking between two teammates can also be carried out in cases where two direct opponents exchange position passing in front of their markers. This solution is shown in Fig. 128

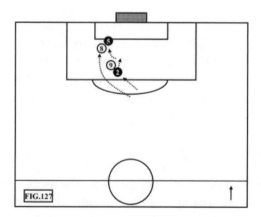

FIG.127

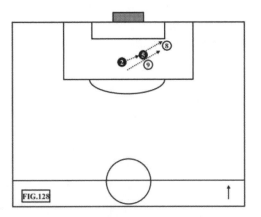

Initially, n° 2 is marking n° 8, and 5 is on 9. When n° 8 makes a crossover with his teammate, the defenders exchange marking.

Practically speaking, this is a defense movement that is also used in situations where the opponents make crossovers. As the movements we are talking about here take place in the danger zone, they will have to be carried out with the right timing and in a coordinated way - leaving even a few meters to the opponents in this zone of the field could be fatal to our team.

AN ANALYSIS OF THE VARIOUS DEAD BALL SITUATIONS

Kick off

The kick off is an important moment in the match, in particular the opening kick off. An organized attitude will immediately give a favorable appearance to the match, especially if you get going with aggression.

As we have already seen when looking at this dead ball situation in attack, there are two possible solutions of play.

- Playing in order to maintain possession with back passes that will allow the team to develop their maneuver;
- Playing in order to go for depth.

In the first case the team has the time to position itself in the right way so as to carry out the chosen defensive strategy. The only problem in the second case is that the defense might find themselves too far forward and the opponents' ball might be chipped over their heads. A possible solution here is not to let the players be deceived by the initial back pass.

Fig. 129 shows the placement of a team fielded with the 4-4-2 in a situation where the opponents are kicking off. The two strikers are on the half way line ready to attack the player that receives the back pass, while the defense positions itself in or around the defending three quarters.

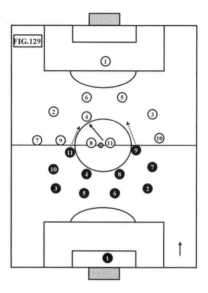

The keeper puts the ball back into play

In this dead ball situation - in particular if the keeper is going for a long clearance - the team must place itself compactly in the central part of the field to regain possession by attacking the ball.

If the keeper makes a short pass, the team should tighten in on the ball using the type of pressing that they have decided to adopt (ultra-offensive, offensive or defensive).

Fig. 130 shows how to position a team fielded with the 4-4-2 and standing by for the keeper to put the ball back into play.

The team will be further into depth or more to the back depending on their estimate of the length of their keeper's kick.

On a long kick, it is best to get the mid field to attack the ball, using the defense section to give coverage.

In such cases you need mid fielders that are good at aerial play, and who are able to attack the ball with the right timing.

Initially the defense will line themselves up in a forward position near the mid field section; and they will then move back as soon as the kick has taken place so as not to concede space to the opposing strikers.

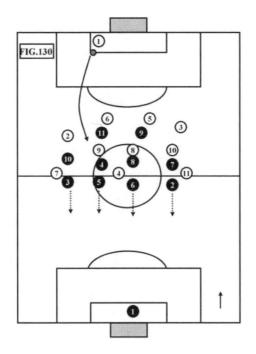

Free kick

You need good organization on a free kick, particularly if it is to be taken in the attacking zone as this is a situation of play that very often puts the defending team in great danger.

The aim is to get numerical superiority in the defense zone, as well as to place the players suitably and to get the marking right.

As we have already seen, the team can use three different defense solutions: the zone, man to man and mixed marking.

The set up when using the zone has been described in Fig. 120.

We must underline again that the defenders have to make the necessary movement backwards and then in to attack the ball.

Mixed marking is very often used, with some players marking particular men and others occupying pre-defined spaces.

Fig. 131 illustrates this solution: it is player n° 9's job to control the space in front of the near post, working on short trajectories; n° 7, on the other hand, operates as a sweeper, and, starting off in a central position, his job is to 'hunt out' the ball in the heart of the area.

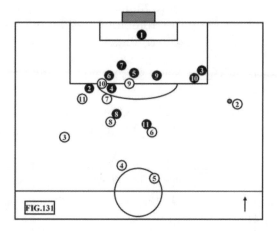

FIG.131

In situations like these you can also place a third player in the space in front of the far post, whose job it will be to work on the long trajectories directed towards this area.

Teammates n° 2, 4, 5 and 6 mark man to man in the center, while n° 8 and 11 have to attack the clearances made by the defense.

The third solution (i.e., man to man marking) has already been illustrated in Fig. 122, but it must be pointed out once again that this type of solution is not very effective.

Generally speaking, it is advisable to line up on a level with the wall, so as not to allow the opposing strikers to come too near the keeper, which would disturb his line of vision and make it more dangerous for him to come out as well as favoring an opponent's deviation.

When the opponents' direct or indirect free kick is to be taken from a central position, you need a good wall to obstruct the shot. The best thing is for the wall to be formed by the tallest players.

If that is not possible, for example, in cases where the wall is made up of four players plus a fifth who will go to meet the ball, the first and the fourth do not need to be tall, whereas height is very important for the second and the third.

The fifth's job is to attack the ball in cases where the free kick is taken by a combination of two players; either that, or he has to go and disturb the player kicking the ball directly, and he must be fast and courageous.

In addition, the wall must remain compact, with all the players acting together.

On direct free kicks, the players making up the wall will have to try and guess from his run up the trajectory that the opponent intends to give the ball: on a hard drive, these four will not jump but will make a slight movement forwards, while if the shot is to be chipped over their heads the wall will have to take a three-quarter step forward, and then jump.

On an indirect free kick, the wall must move to the side to cover the goal better with respect to the point from which the next shot will be coming.

In cases where the free kick is taken from a position to the back, having first evaluated the strength of the opponent's drive, it is best to keep the opposing team as far away as possible from our goal, placing the defense line high up so as not to concede depth, and then bringing it back when the player taking the kick has begun his run up. All this is independent of the type of marking in use.

You can see this type of situation in Fig. 132.

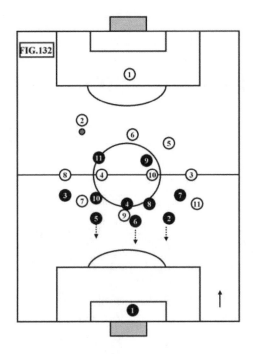

Corner kick

Once again, corners are dangerous, and the coach will have to organize the defense to be used on them with care and determination.

The three solutions that we have already considered above are all possible on corners. In a team that is using zonal defense on a corner you expect all the players to defend, starting off from pre-determined positions and occupying a pre-defined space.

In addition, each player has the job of attacking the ball and looking after the space assigned to him.

Using zonal defense on corner kicks means giving priority to covering the spaces and to evaluating the trajectories of the crosses.

Fig. 133 shows the placement of a team that is using zonal defense on a corner kick taken from the right.

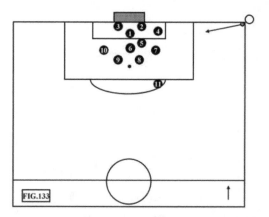

N° 4 occupies the space between the near post and the edge of the goal area. This is a delicate position from which you have to attack the short, fast trajectories, as well as anticipating any player who might try to flick the ball on. As far as individual skills are concerned, if the n° 4 is to do his work he must be good at anticipating both with his head and with his feet, and he does not need to be tall. N° 2 and 3 take up position on the two posts, ready to help the keeper with his saves and cover the goal when he goes out. You do not need to be tall in these positions, but it is a good idea for the two players to have their strong foot towards the inside of the goal.

N° 10 occupies the space in front of the far post. He must control this zone with great attention, because the ball will very often arrive here, both directly on the cross and following flick on shots. In this position you need players that are tall and heavily built.

Player n° 7 occupies the space in front of the near post, vertically out from the zone controlled by the n° 4. N° 7 has the same tasks and skills as n° 4.

Players n° 5, 6, 8 and 9 control the central space going from the edge of the goal area to the edge of the penalty area. This is a very dangerous zone for the defense because it is in a central position, it is fairly near the goal and it is a sizeable space which will generally be attacked by opposing players who are good at aerial play.

For these reasons, the four players must be good at aerial play. They must also be tall and heavily built, and need good personality and courage.

N° 11 works in the part of the field that includes the edge of the penalty area and the penalty arc. In this zone of the field you need good tactical skill. This player must put a stop to playing schemes that lead to the opponents shooting from outside the area, and he must attack any long clearances and take possession of short deflections.

With his teammates positioned in this way, the keeper will be better able to come out on trajectories to the center of the area.

As far as defensive solutions with mixed marking are concerned, we have already had a look at them in Fig. 121.

The last option - i.e., man to man marking - is rarely used because of the few advantages that it brings.

In any case, Fig. 134 is an illustration of such a solution.

Player n° 6 takes up position on the post, while all the others mark their direct opponent.

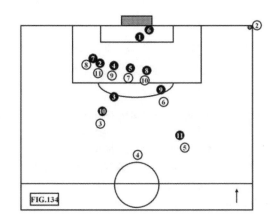

FIG.134

The throw in

As a result of the sheer number of times it actually happens and the greater and greater attention it is receiving in the attacking phase, the throw in has taken on an important role, and therefore requires special training in order to organize it as effectively as possible.

The limited space that it is generally possible to cover with a throw gives a great advantage to the defending team, which can effectively reduce the opponents' playing space and time.

To do that, it is necessary to create numerical superiority in the zone where the throw in is being taken, without neglecting your defensive balance.

You must have the right attitude in connection to the zone of the field where the ball is to be thrown in.

You can see in Fig. 135 the zones of the field in which you will have to diversify your defensive attitude.

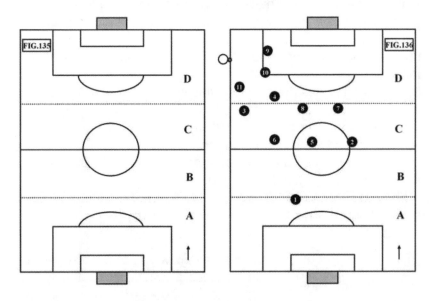

The first thing to underline is that the team must stay compact during the defense phase and that the players must stay as short and tight as possible, independently of the system or the type of marking they are using. A throw in from zone D gives the defenders the advantage of being near the opponents' goal if they gain possession. The half way line sets an important limit to the depth of the defenders, who will thus be better able to manage the danger of an in-depth attack (there is an illustration of this situation in Fig. 136, the team fielded with a 4-4-2).

A throw in from zone C can be dangerous because if you choose to create numerical superiority near the ball, the defense will have to keep forward in order to shorten up the team, leaving a good space behind that not even the keeper will be able to reduce.

To avoid this disadvantage it is a good idea to position the defense and the mid field a little further back, and the strikers wide.

This kind of attitude will limit your chances of putting pressure on the opponents, but it will make it easier for you to manage an in-depth attack.

Fig. 137 shows how to line up the 4-4-2 in a thrown in situation in zone C.

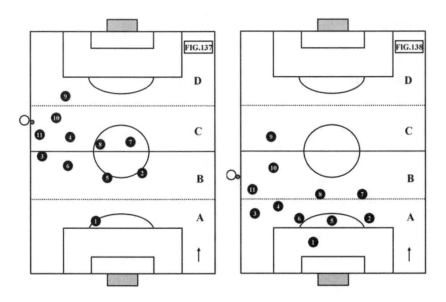

Zone B is the part of the field that will allow you to put the greatest pressure on your opponents because it is difficult to attack from this position into depth (and now even the keeper will be giving a hand). You will have great numerical superiority around the ball, but, as you get nearer to the goal, the number of defending players must be reduced so as to get tighter control of the objective to be defended. This defense solution in zone B is illustrated in Fig. 138.

Throw ins carried out in zone A force the team to change their defensive objectives. Defending the goal becomes the priority rather than defensive concentration around the ball. You will have to be very careful about long throw ins to the center of the area, which can lead to direct shots on goal or dangerous flick on headers. In this zone of the field the diagonals of reciprocal coverage have disappeared, and the team sections are flattened out around the goal.

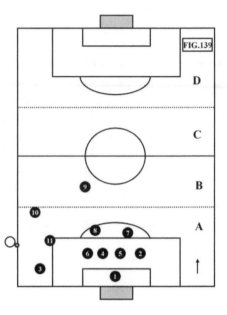

Fig. 139 shows the positions of a team defending with the 4-4-2 on a throw in from zone A.

Penalty kicks

Naturally, this is a dead ball situation with a high scoring percentage for the team in attack. The keeper has most of the responsibility in defense, and he is now the last blockade in defense. A good number (preferably eight) of the other defenders should occupy the space at the limit of the area, and it is their job to cut out the direct opponents, immediately attacking the ball after the keeper's clearance, or if it rebounds off the post. You can see in Fig 140 how to place the team on a penalty to be taken by the opponents.

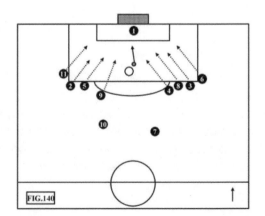

Conclusions

In conclusion, I think it is important to underline yet again the growing importance of dead ball situations in modern soccer.

Teams in every category have reached high levels of playing organization, and this forces all modern coaches who wish to train with method and productivity to dedicate a lot of time to set plays both in attack and defense.

I hope to have made a contribution that can be used as a stepping stone towards other considerations, as a basis from which to begin for all those who want to give their team effective organization of play even in these fundamental situations.

Of course, each coach will have to put the subjects we have treated into the context of his own needs, finalizing them to the characteristics of his players and to the subjective condition of the team.

It is equally important for the coach to confront and talk to his players so that they can find together the attacking and defending solutions on dead balls that will give greatest safety, making sure that everyone is in agreement on what is to be done.

A relationship that allows for constructive discussion will enable you to adopt defensive and attacking plays that are effective as well as productive.

My final hope is to have given concrete aid to all those coaches that have chosen to read this book, sure that soccer as it is played is going in a direction that leads to greater and greater collective organization, which in turn brings to light the individual skills of the players themselves.

Marco Ceccomori